The Development of Western Civilization

*Narrative Essays in the History of Our Tradition from
Its Origins in Ancient Israel and Greece to the Present*

Edited by Edward W. Fox
*Professor of Modern European History
Cornell University*

THE AGE OF ADVERSITY
The Fourteenth Century

By ROBERT E. LERNER

"Boniface VIII Proclaiming the Jubilee," from *All the Paintings of Giotto*, Part I; reproduced by permission of Hawthorne Books, Inc.

THE

AGE OF ADVERSITY

The Fourteenth Century

ROBERT E. LERNER

NORTHWESTERN UNIVERSITY

Cornell University Press

ITHACA, NEW YORK

Foreword

THE proposition that each generation must rewrite history is more widely quoted than practiced. In the field of college texts on Western civilization, the conventional accounts have been revised, and sources and supplementary materials have been developed; but it is too long a time since the basic narrative has been rewritten to meet the rapidly changing needs of new college generations. In the mid-twentieth century such an account must be brief, well written, and based on unquestioned scholarship and must assume almost no previous historical knowledge on the part of the reader. It must provide a coherent analysis of the development of Western civilization and its basic values. It must, in short, constitute a systematic introduction to the collective memory of that tradition which we are being asked to defend. This series of narrative essays was undertaken in an effort to provide such a text for an introductory history survey course and is being published in the present form in the belief that the requirements of that one course reflected a need that is coming to be widely recognized.

Now that the classic languages, the Bible, the great historical novels, even most non-American history, have dropped out of the normal college preparatory program, it is imperative that a text in the history of European civilization be fully self-explanatory. This means not only that it must begin at the beginning, with the origins of our civilization in ancient Israel and Greece, but that it must introduce every name or event that takes an integral place in the account and ruthlessly delete all others no matter how firmly imbedded in historical protocol. Only thus simplified and complete will the narrative present a sufficiently clear outline of those major trends and developments that have led from the beginning of our recorded time to the most pressing of our current problems. This simplification, however, need not involve intellectual dilution or evasion. On the contrary, it can effectively raise rather than lower the level of presentation. It is on this assumption that the present series has been based, and each contributor has been urged to write for a mature and literate audience. It is hoped, therefore, that the essays may also prove profitable and rewarding to readers outside the college classroom.

The plan of the first part of the series is to sketch, in related essays, the narrative of our history from its origins to the eve of the French Revolution; each is being written by a recognized scholar and is designed to serve as the basic reading for one week in a semester course. The developments of the nineteenth and twentieth centuries will be covered in a succeeding series which will provide the same quantity of reading material for each week of the second semester. This scale of presentation has been adopted in a conviction that any understanding of the central problem of the preservation of the integrity and dignity of the individual human being depends first on an examination of the origins of our tradition in the politics and philosophy of the ancient Greeks and the religion of the ancient Hebrews and then on a relatively more detailed knowledge of its recent development within our industrial urban society.

The decision to devote equal space to twenty-five centuries and to a century and a half was based on the analogy with the human memory. Those events most remote tend to be remembered in least detail but often with a sense of clarity and perspective that is absent in more recent and more crowded recollections. If the roots of our tradition must be identified, their relation to the present must be carefully developed. The nearer the narrative approaches contemporary times, the more difficult and complicated this becomes. Recent experience must be worked over more thoroughly and in more detail if it is to contribute effectively to an understanding of the contemporary world.

It may be objected that the series attempts too much. The attempt is being made, however, on the assumption that any historical development should be susceptible of meaningful treatment on any scale and in the realization that a very large proportion of today's college students do not have more time to invest in this part of their education. The practical alternative appears to lie between some attempt to create a new brief account of the history of our tradition and the abandonment of any serious effort to communicate the essence of that tradition to all but a handful of our students. It is the conviction of everyone contributing to this series that the second alternative must not be accepted by default.

In a series covering such a vast sweep of time, few scholars would find themselves thoroughly at home in the fields covered by more than one or two of the essays. This means, in practice, that almost every essay should be written by a different author. In spite of apparent drawbacks, this procedure promises real advantages. Each contributor will be in a position to set higher standards of accuracy and insight in an essay encompassing a major portion of the field of his life's work than could ordinarily be expected in surveys of some ten or twenty centuries. The inevitable discontinuity of style and interpretation could be modified by editorial coordination; but it was felt that some discontinuity was in itself desirable. No illusion is more easily acquired by the student in an elementary course, or is more prejudicial to the efficacy of such a course, than that a single smoothly articulated text represents the very substance of history itself. If the shift from author to author, week by week, raises difficulties for the beginning student, they are difficulties that will not so much impede his progress as contribute to his growth.

In this essay, *The Age of Adversity*, Mr. Robert E. Lerner has summarized the history of Europe in the fourteenth century. Overshadowed by the dazzling achievements of the preceding and succeeding centuries, the fourteenth has tended to be neglected as a period of irrelevant misfortune and confusion. Famine followed by plague compounded by war wrought havoc scarcely equaled in European experience; but Mr. Lerner demonstrates that the history of the age was no mere product of tragic accidents. Before these struck, the character of the period had been established by the crumbling and collapse of overextended aims of the thirteenth century. And after the disasters had done their worst, their victims still struggled, undaunted, to defend their world. Where they had been unable to triumph over the tremendous odds against which they contended, they still managed to survive by resilience and resourcefulness. Those institutions and values they could not preserve intact, they readapted to the cataclysmic changes, thus, inadvertently, initiating a series of innovations that were to bear fruit in new, tougher social structures and clearer, more realistic insights. In this account of the response of men of the fourteenth century to the challenge of adversity, we can now discern the distinct if remote origins of some of the most fundamental patterns of our own ways of thought and action.

The author and editor wish to express their gratitude for helpful suggestions to Mr. Joseph R. Strayer and Mr. Anthony Molho.

EDWARD WHITING FOX

Ithaca, New York
May 1967

Contents

Foreword, by Edward Whiting Fox   v

Introduction   1

I   Catastrophe   7

II   Struggle   35

III   Triumph   81

Epilogue   119

Chronological Summary   123

Suggestions for Further Reading   126

Index   131

Introduction

POPE BONIFACE VIII, the last great representative of the mediaeval papacy, had a taste for the extravagant. This penchant for acting on a grand scale brought him varying results throughout a long career, and ultimately contributed to his defeat and death. At no point, however, did his extravagance find more appropriate expression than in his proclamation of the first papal jubilee at Rome in the year 1300.

The scene is preserved in a retouched and badly damaged fresco, probably by the Italian painter Giotto, which depicts Boniface adorned with the splendid papal tiara and mantle standing on a balcony of the Vatican basilica between two cardinals. Directly before him hangs the bull of jubilee framed by draperies decorated with his family arms. Below, presumably, is an immense crowd assembled to receive the announcement that during that year those who, in a true state of penitence, visited the basilicas of St. Peter and St. Paul for fifteen days—or thirty for native Romans—would receive pardon for their sins.

In response to this unprecedented proclamation, the faithful poured into Rome from all parts of Italy and beyond the Alps, on horseback and on foot, with the aged and decrepit borne on the shoulders of their children. The exact number of pilgrims is impossible to determine, but one eye-witness declared that throughout the year there were never less than 200,000 foreigners in the city and the rumor persisted that 2,000,000 pilgrims had passed through Rome by the end of the year. Even granting that these figures must have been inflated in the usual mediaeval manner, the impression created, as one chronicler noted, was that "almost the whole world was running to the Roman Curia."

The reasons for this extraordinary success were undoubtedly complex. If the concept of drawing on the papal treasury of merits for the pardon of sins had been evolving for centuries, the idea of a special occasion for its exercise was new, unexpected, and appealing. And Rome itself still provided a tremendous attraction for pilgrims and tourists as the shrine of the greatest martyrs, the seat of the papacy, and the traditional capital of the world. Even so, the basic object of the jubilee, the public celebration of the apogee of papal authority and majesty in the pontificate of Boniface, must be counted a major factor in the triumph.

Some reflection of this emotional response may be seen or sensed in the works of three budding celebrities—all from Florence—whose names were destined to grace the pages of history. The young Giotto probably made his first trip to Rome to participate in the preparations for the jubilee and to paint the fresco which recorded the scene described above. He was followed by the scholar Giovanni Villani, who declared the jubilee "the most marvelous scene ever witnessed," and who was so stirred by the history he read in the monuments of Rome that he decided to write a chronicle of his own city, which as *The History of Florence* was to become one of the greatest of all mediaeval historical writings in the vernacular. Finally, the famous description by Dante of pilgrims to the jubilee crossing the bridge to St. Peter's is so vivid as to suggest that he too must have been present at the celebration. In any case, the fact that he set the *Divine Comedy* in the year 1300 would seem to demonstrate his preoccupation with the symbolic significance of the year of jubilee.

Nor was this surprising. At the time, while Boniface was celebrating the jubilee, most Europeans could have been as satisfied with their accomplishments and their prospects as was the Pope with his. The political, economic, and cultural advances of the preceding two centuries, the greatest since the fall of the Roman Empire, contributed not merely to a sense of satisfaction but to confidence in the future. The enthusiasm for the papal triumph, however, was not universal as could have been inferred from the failure of the great secular authorities, the German Emperor and the kings of France and England, to make an appearance at Rome.

At the time, it is true, Edward I of England, Philip IV of France, and the German Emperor Albert of Hapsburg were all occupied with serious problems at home; and the first two, at least, sent emissaries to represent them at Rome. But neither the chronic unrest of their vassals nor unresolved issues between themselves would have been likely to keep Edward and Philip from Rome if they had not both been involved with Boniface in a major struggle for prestige and power. The Emperor, it might be added, was detained in Germany by intrigues fomented by Pope Boniface himself, who was attempting to assert and even to exercise supreme lay power. To have attended the jubilee might well have given the reigning monarchs the sense of celebrating the triumph of an authority they were preparing to resist to the limit of their resources.

In 1296, Boniface VIII had issued a bull, *Clericis laicos,* forbidding secular rulers to levy taxes on the clergy without the Pope's consent. A direct challenge to the kings of France and England, it provoked a vigorous reaction from both Philip IV and Edward I. Boniface appeared to retreat, but in 1302 he returned to the attack with the bull *Unam sanctam,* in which he announced that "it is entirely necessary for salvation that all human creation be subject to the pope of Rome." Even if, as is now held, the ideas expressed were not new, the tone and manner of their expression were. After a futile attempt at negotiation, Philip sent one of his principal advisers, Guillaume de Nogaret, to arrest the Pope and bring him to France for trial before a council to be summoned for the purpose. Nogaret found Boniface at a country residence at Anagni, where he subjected the aged and ailing pontiff to threats and humiliations so extreme as to arouse the townspeople to his defense. Nogaret retreated, but a short while later Boniface died of shock. The real outcome of the confrontation, however, can be seen in the election, in 1305, of Clement V to the papacy. Archbishop of Bordeaux, he never did go to Rome, but instead set up his court at Avignon, a papal enclave in southeastern France, thus becoming a virtual, if voluntary, pawn of Philip. Seldom in history has such pride as Boniface expressed in 1300 at the jubilee been followed so swiftly by such a total fall.

His was the tragedy of a brilliant but deeply flawed character. It was also the climax of a long, mounting conflict between spiritual and secular authority in mediaeval society. And most important, in this context, it symbolized the destruction of the great thirteenth-century synthesis—which had reached its political culmination in the middle of the century—

by the unchecked extension of its inner principles to ultimate and disastrous conclusions. In spite of many personal conflicts between individual rulers, the authority of Rome, at least in theory, supported and balanced that of the kings or emperor, just as both lay and secular powers were nourished by the freely given financial support of the towns. The harmonious and balanced interaction of these forces had produced the great political structures of the age. Attempts to transform each into independent and unlimited powers could only end in general political disruption and in the destruction or transformation of each institution.

If Boniface was one of the first and most spectacular victims of this process, he was not the last. Although Edward I of England, Philip IV of France, and the Emperor Albert of Hapsburg appeared to their contemporaries as particularly capable and successful rulers, they too were to be swept rapidly from the scene and Europe was not to know their like again for generations. At first glance the lack of capable successors might appear a mere accident of inheritance; neither Philip IV nor Edward I left sons of character or ability comparable to his own. But a close look at the history of the ensuing years reveals that if these rulers' heirs were inferior, the problems they faced were new and ominous.

CHAPTER I

Catastrophe

IN the folklore of western Europe there is a legend of a sunken bell that had once been the pulse of a vigorous community, tolling off periods of work and calling people to worship. As a result of an act of God, however, the life of the town was cut short by plague, fire, or flood—according to the particular version—and its inhabitants destroyed or scattered, its streets delivered over to ghosts. Nothing was left except the mournful toll of the abandoned or sunken bell, which could still be heard by passing travelers during the late hours of the night. If legend is the product of folk imagination, the roots of this one lie deep in historical experience, for during the fourteenth century villages were left deserted throughout large sections of the continent.

The Problems of Saturation

The history of fourteenth-century Europe is perhaps best explained in terms of the widely held theory that economies that cease to expand begin to contract.

Mediaeval history is, from an economic point of view, the story of a general expansion that began about the year 1000 and continued at an accelerating rate for some three hundred years. During this period, population multiplied, trade expanded, new towns were founded, and huge areas of land were reclaimed for cultivation.

By the late thirteenth century, many sectors of the European economy began to show signs of having reached a saturation point. With such a vast subject as the economic life of Europe, it is impossible to establish a precise date of transition. Not only did circumstances vary greatly from country to country, but certain spheres of economic life continued to expand until well into the fourteenth century, while others had already begun to contract before it began. In addition, the documentary evidence is so confusing and even contradictory that trained economic historians often find themselves disagreeing about some of the most basic generalizations. Most, however, will agree that by the middle of the fourteenth century western Europe was undergoing a severe economic crisis.

It is almost never possible to determine just what reverses the momentum of the expanding economic cycle and turns it downward; but in the late thirteenth century one example of the effect of overexpansion can be identified. In the early Middle Ages, the large mass of peasants lived essentially as subsistence farmers on self-contained manors. In the twelfth and thirteenth centuries, however, there was a marked increase in population. When the manors became crowded, people left the land for the towns. As these in turn filled up, a large number of new ones were created providing a growing and, by the standards of the time, an apparently unlimited market for grain. This new demand could be met only by a substantial increase of production. New land was needed, and new hands to work it. As a result, still more overflow population from the manors began to open areas that had hitherto been considered unpromising for cultivation. Because the topsoil of the river valleys of northwestern Europe and southeastern England is rich, deep, and all but inexhaustible, mediaeval society had managed to survive, even prosper, with crude agricultural methods. But applied to the new marginal lands these traditional methods produced profitable results only for the first few years and in the process exhausted the poor soil. It is a classic story, repeated as recently as the 1920's in the American Midwest. By 1300, many of the "colonists" found they could no longer count on adequate crops and began to abandon their recently reclaimed farms. At the same time, improved farming methods combined with more intensive efforts applied to both old and new lands led to the production of a surplus with its inevitable concomitant falling prices. In the meantime, in the towns, similar developments were taking place. Thus, just as a disastrous downward trend in agricultural prices was bringing the reclamation of land to an abrupt halt, and laborers were leaving exhausted fields to seek work elsewhere, employment in the towns was becoming more and more difficult to find.

The Problems of Adversity

To add to the basic problem of overexpansion and saturation, western Europeans were faced with a series of calamities beyond their control. Because agriculture was still the dominant source of livelihood and because Europeans had not devised adequate techniques for storing food, the vagaries of climate, particularly rainfall, had an overwhelming effect on everyday life. Famine, endemic during the Middle Ages, assumed catastrophic proportions in the fourteenth century. A disastrous crop failure, for example, occurred in 1315, when summer rainfall became a deluge so constant and widespread that chroniclers compared it to the flood in the seventh chapter of Genesis. Crops were ruined from one end of Europe to the other, from Scotland and Russia in the north to Spain and Italy in the south, and the resulting famine was so severe in some areas that there were reports of people eating their own children. Hunger not only drove men to crime, it left them vulnerable to disease, and it threatened the social order. Apocalyptic prophecies were rife, anticipating or perhaps provoking such uprisings as that of the French shep-

herds or *Pastoureaux*. The harvest was abundant in
1316, but the damage was too great to be repaired in
a single year. Serious shortages continued in many
parts of Europe until 1317 and even longer in Poland
and Silesia, where as late as 1319 it was reported that
bodies of criminals were taken from the gallows and
eaten by the poor.

The floods that caused the famine of 1315 were to
become a recurrent problem in the fourteenth century. In Holland, for example, they exceeded in de-
structiveness anything known in the twelfth or thirteenth centuries. In 1333, a terrible flood washed out
the bridges of Florence, inflicting on that city the
greatest natural disaster it had ever suffered. The climate not only became wetter; a study of glaciers in
Greenland, Iceland, and Norway suggests that it also
became significantly colder as well, thus accounting
for the southward shift of the tree line in Scandinavia.
And the cumulative effect of all these factors was to
put a halt to economic expansion and to initiate a
period of retrenchment.

This trend was reinforced by the contraction of
trade routes—another development beyond the control of western Europeans. The last important Christians ports in the Holy Land—Acre, Tyre, Beirut,
Sidon, and Tortosa—fell to the Moslems in 1291. At
the same time, the Mongols, who had brought with
them relative peace and favorable trading conditions,
began to lose their control of the trade routes leading

to the Levant. The Ottoman Turks filled the vacuum left by the Mongol disintegration. In 1354 they had made their first beachhead in Europe, and by the end of the century they controlled the Balkans. A Western crusading army which tried to turn them back was defeated at Nicopolis in 1396, and only the short-lived revival of certain Mongol tribes under the celebrated Tamerlaine was able to check the Ottoman advance. But the situation was not really improved by Tamerlaine's Mongols, who left behind them a swath of devastation, in which "was heard neither barking of dog, nor cackling of fowl, nor cry of child." These disturbances in the East sharply curtailed the flourishing trade of the thirteenth century. In 1343, for example, a characteristic war between the Mongols and the Genoese in the Crimea caused a 50 to 100 per cent rise in the price of spices. The Ottomans themselves were not hostile to trade, but they were considerably less pliant than the weak Byzantine and Asiatic potentates who had ruled the area before.

Another malignant influence was the chronic war that plagued Europe and the Levant. Wars were fought among Italian cities, German princedoms, northern trading powers, and western monarchies. There were also the smaller civil wars—town against country, class against class, clan against clan. Some of the most famous conflicts of history—from the Hundred Years' War between England and France to the family war between the Montagues and Capulets—belong to this period. In fact, taking these together with the even more numerous struggles lost in the confusion of its history, the fourteenth century suffered from more, bloodier, and longer wars than any since the tenth. The inevitable profiteering and speculation created and dissipated unstable fortunes with lightning speed and disastrous consequences. In time, this instability brought even the most solidly established firms to bankruptcy. A defaulted English war debt, for example, finally brought down the prestigious, but overextended, Florentine banking houses of the Bardi and Peruzzi, causing widespread economic hardship in all of Italy. Only the arms industry thrived, while peaceful enterprise languished in the ruined towns and desolated countryside.

The Black Death

Devastating as all these misfortunes were, there is a possibility that Europeans might have been able to overcome them by retrenchment and adjustment. They were, at least in exaggerated form, the common stuff of mediaeval life, which has made some historians unwilling to employ so categorical a term as "depression" to the tribulations of the first half of the fourteenth century. For the second half, however, such circumspection would be utterly inappropriate. In 1347, Europe was all but overwhelmed by a new calamity which far exceeded anything yet experienced in the West in either its impact or its extent.

The Black Death, or bubonic plague, entered Europe through the city of Constantinople. From there, it was transhipped along the trade routes that converged on the ports until it engulfed all of Europe. The disease had never been seen before and the medical profession was helpless to combat it. Nearly everyone who was infected fell with horrifying dispatch. Because of crowded and unsanitary conditions, towns suffered more than the countryside and the poor suffered more than the rich. The infection was no respecter of persons, but the young and vigorous seem to have fallen in undue proportion and the wealthy were by no means immune. From Italy to England it raged in full fury through 1348 and 1349, and then spread in the following years as far as Greenland, Iceland, and Russia. Then, after a brief respite, it became a constantly reappearing phenomenon, returning in the sixties, the seventies, and at later periodic intervals as if to complete a job unfinished.

To estimate the mortality rate of the Black Death one must indulge in a large amount of guesswork, for accurate data are unavailable. Contemporaries cited figures which have to be dismissed as products of hysteria, but even so scholars now generally agree that the death rate varied from twenty to fifty per hundred depending on the area. The population of Florence and Siena, for example, seems to have been cut by half during the summer months of 1348 alone, while that of Bristol, England, was reduced by 35 to 40 per cent. Some towns escaped unscathed while others were totally destroyed. Even if the overall figure was "only" a quarter of the European population, the plague still killed a far greater percentage of the population than has any war—including those of the twentieth century. To describe the setting for his *Decameron*, Boccaccio reproduced, without attribution, Thucydides' account of the disposal of the dead during the plague in Athens: "They dug for each graveyard a huge trench in which they laid the corpses as they arrived by hundreds at a time, piling them up tier by tier as merchandise is stowed in a ship and throwing in a little earth until they were filled to the top."

The Black Death had a more decisive influence on the economy than all the earlier calamities combined. Famine and war tend to reduce population and food supply at roughly the same rate, but plague destroys the population without touching goods or property. Thus, while hamlets and towns were emptied, barns and warehouses remained full. The sheep roamed freely in the sheepfolds for lack of shepherds and wheat rotted in the fields for lack of reapers. The inevitable result was a tremendous oversupply of goods, an even greater contraction of markets, and an acute shortage of labor.

Some segments of society actually benefited from

this development. Prices dropped while the supply of money per capita increased. At the same time, because of the shortage of labor, salaries rose so sharply that, in the country, many serfs were able to buy their freedom. The lords were forced to make this concession and others in order to retain their agricultural workers, who were being lured to the towns by all manner of inducements, including personal freedom. As a result, the period is frequently designated as the golden age of wage labor.

But these blessings were far from unmixed. Landlords were badly hurt by the plummeting prices of grain and any remaining profits were eaten up by the sharply rising wages. Moreover, the customary dues that landlords had always received for the use of their mills and presses were reduced as the plague robbed the lords of their tenants. Nor could this loss be made up by raising rents and fees. Not only were these usually fixed by tradition and therefore difficult to alter, but even when they could be changed, they offered little help since any increase would make it even harder to attract and hold labor. The most obvious—and common—expedient, then, to compensate for the decline of income was to reduce the amount of cultivation.

Townsfolk too, while less severely hurt, were also affected. The agricultural crisis tended to drive peasants to the towns, where prices were still low and wages high. As a result, the condition of the working population was frequently more prosperous than ever before. Unfortunately, however, there was no solid base for this improvement, since the decisive economic factor in the towns as in the country was the shrinking of markets. Manufacturers and entrepreneurs could no more afford to continue paying high wages than the landlords, since their goods too had to be sold at lower and lower prices. Even reduced production saturated the dwindling markets and choked the economy. The instinctive reaction in both town and country was to "crack down" on labor with restrictive legislation. Instead of attempting to develop new markets, an undertaking which seemed quite hopeless, the different economic groups struggled with one another for a larger share of the diminishing income, and the fourteenth century exhausted itself in some of the most bitter and destructive class warfare to be seen in Europe before the Industrial Revolution.

Agriculture and Industry

Viewed in the perspective of European history rather than in its immediate impact, the depression of the fourteenth century displays an irregular and sharply oscillating pattern of wages, prices, and gross product. But if certain areas of the economy flourished and the living standards of many rose, actually the total economy contracted and declined.

One positive result of the population decline, as

we have seen above, was the breaking of servile bonds. The sudden reduction of the population completed the work of previous centuries by freeing most of the serfs in both western and eastern Europe; and the cruel hardships of the period at least bore the fruit of positive social progress. Because farming had become so much less profitable, huge patches of marginal land that could not bear the strain of constant cultivation were returned to wilderness. Although it has been said that "in the history of land problems there is no sin like the sin of generalization," there were few exceptions to this pattern of abandoned holdings throughout western Europe. Parts of Germany were the most severely affected. In the southwest, for example, the rate of abandonment ran to more than half, and in sections of the Austrian Alps and the Black Forest the population is still sparser today than it was before the plague.

In an economy dominated by agriculture, an agricultural depression was bound to affect all other spheres of enterprise, and often the impact was increased by other factors. In the mining industry, for example, the depression coincided with a depletion of ores, notably of silver and copper. Only iron seemed to have escaped the slump, partly because it was more easily obtainable and partly because of the constant demand for weapons of war. The exhaustion of silver, however, complicated by the chronic drainage of European money to the East, caused an acute scarcity of bullion that led in turn to a widespread debasement of the coinage. Not only were there constant complaints about this monetary chaos, but as the discovery of coin hoards demonstrates, men hastened to hide good coins underground.

The woolen and cloth industry also suffered from the general instability and stagnation, but in this instance losses in some areas contributed to gains in others. Because of constant war, decreasing demand, increasing duties, and savage competition, the foreign sale of English wool—once the country's basic export—was sharply curtailed. It has been estimated that in the early fourteenth century the average export of English wool reached 35,000 sacks per year, but that by the mid-fifteenth century the figure had fallen to 8,000. This decline of trade in raw wool, however, was compensated for by an accompanying increase in its manufacture into cloth, which was stimulated by a technological revolution in fulling—the process of shrinking woolen cloth. The new techniques were based on the power of water mills and proved to be more efficient than the primitive methods of beating the cloth with clubs or trampling it under foot. The use of water mills also tended to disperse industry over the English countryside, which not only helped check the flight of labor to the towns but also enabled the manufacturers to escape the restrictive controls of city guilds. This transformation of the cloth trade was a first step in the long-term process of English industrialization.

As the English cloth industry prospered, that in

Flanders declined. Once one of the most advanced segments of mediaeval economy, it suffered severely during the fourteenth century from social unrest, war, the declining supply of English wool, and the new competition of finished cloth from England. In most instances the results of these pressures were catastrophic. The city of Ypres, which had once been a flourishing center of manufacture, saw its population drop from roughly 20,000 in the early fourteenth century to 8,000 by the end of the fifteenth century. The great Flemish city of Bruges managed to maintain its pre-eminence by its mercantile activity, but even Bruges was often crippled by social unrest and vain efforts to curb the competition of English cloth by the prohibition of English imports. By the end of the fifteenth century, the embargo on English cloth so reduced Bruges' total trade as to contribute to the rise of its rival Antwerp. Finally Bruges' long decline was completed by the silting up of its river.

It is not possible here to discuss the varied fortunes of manufacture and trade in all other parts of Europe, but it should be noted that even northern Italy, the most prosperous area of fourteenth-century Europe, suffered sharp fluctuations in its production and income. Thanks to advanced business techniques, however, Italy was able to siphon off a large percentage of European wealth during this period, a practice which accounts for the cordial dislike felt by northern Europeans for most Italians. Even in areas like France and Germany, where manufacturing was less developed, the economic crisis left its mark. In Germany it brought about an exodus from the countryside that produced a golden age for towns. Splendid town halls were built and universities were founded, but in their shadow a large urban populace lived on the edge of destitution and despair.

Economic Alliances

In the first half of the fourteenth century, sharply fluctuating prices helped speculators amass huge individual fortunes. When the English crown defaulted on its debt to the Bardi and Peruzzi banks of Florence, English bankers reaped large returns by stepping into the breach and financing the war, while others made quick profits from the burgeoning cloth trade. But the instability of the age destroyed fortunes as quickly as it created them; and in the long run, it was not great speculators but conservative and responsible men who flourished. Among the attempts to lessen the devastating effects of depression, the formation of trade alliances yielded the most uniformly rewarding results.

The most famous of these was the Hanse or Hanseatic League of northern Germany. Throughout the thirteenth century, merchants from the German ports had plied the waters of the North Sea and the Baltic. Working in close cooperation, they had, by the end of the century, established extraterritorial enclaves in London, Bruges, Bergen, and Novgorod. The pressures of the following century, however, transformed this informal system into a tightly knit alliance. By the middle of the fourteenth century, the informal league of merchants depended on the support of the governments of their respective cities—notably Lübeck, Hamburg, Bremen, Wismar, and Rostock. This league was cemented by outside threats. When the King of Denmark tried to limit German traffic between the North Sea and the Baltic in 1367, the league of Hanseatic cities opened hostilities in defense of their merchants and trade. As a result, the Hanse won a resounding victory, sealed by the Peace of Stralsund in 1370, and gained control of the important timber, fish, and grain trade of the North. By the beginning of the fifteenth century, it not only dominated the Baltic but monopolized the trade with Poland, Russia, and large portions of Scandinavia. Indeed, the prestige of the Hanse was so great that Lübeck, Hamburg, and Bremen are still proud to call themselves Hanseatic cities and to perpetuate the Hanseatic initials on their automobile license plates as a reminder of their great tradition.

The success of the Hanse set a trend toward economic nationalism and monopoly throughout Europe. In England, a company of merchants known as the Staple was established by a royal grant to regulate the wool trade. If the first purpose of the grant was to collect taxes for the crown, it also served—at the cost of some restriction of trade—to provide a steady income for the members and to limit the possibility of unscrupulous speculation. After operating by turns from the leading cities of the Low Countries, it finally found, in 1363, a fixed seat in Calais, which had the advantage, for the crown, of being an English possession. Similar staples were established for tin, lead, and cloth.

The shrinking markets and increasing competition which characterized the depression encouraged the development of rational business methods. In fact some historians think that the advanced techniques of banking, bookkeeping, and business which were developed during this period provided the essentials for the birth of capitalism. Others, however, would point out that it takes more than mere institutions to make capitalism and would argue that the essential acquisitive spirit was still lacking in the fourteenth century. But if the capitalistic spirit was not fully present, one still cannot ignore the structural innovations which, together with the persistent courage of those who struggled to make a living, clearly contributed to the revival of the European economy by the second half of the fifteenth century.

Social Upheaval

The fourteenth century was an age of insecurity, in social as well as economic relations. Its history is dominated by nearly constant insurrection and upheaval and also records an obsession with social status and stability unprecedented in the earlier history of mediaeval society.

From the very beginning of the century, acute social unrest threatened the more populous and industrialized areas of Flanders and northern Italy. In these regions the workers were at the mercy of entrepreneurs who both supplied their raw materials and sold their finished products. Frustrated by declining prices and dwindling markets and tempted by the shortage of labor, these city workers maintained a constant struggle with the artisans and patricians. As early as 1302, this discontent flared up in Flanders in the so-called "Matins of Bruges," in which the populace revolted, destroying the French garrison that defended the interests of the patricians. In retaliation, the King of France sent a large army to teach the rebels a lesson, but it was he himself who was taught. At Courtrai, the royal army was decisively defeated by a host of Flemish workers led by a poor weaver of Bruges. This startling victory, however, did not put an end either to social privilege or conflict. The upper classes managed to return to power and the brutal class struggle continued throughout the century.

In Italy, the most noteworthy uprising of the lower classes occurred in Florence. There, poor workmen known as *Ciompi*, primarily of the woolen industry, were prevented by Florentine law from forming guilds and thus denied any voice in the city's government. In desperation, in the summer of 1378, they resorted to a series of violent riots and seized temporary control of the city. But even though they succeeded in forming their own government, their movement split, after a few short weeks, into moderate and extremist factions. To destroy the extremists, the moderates then made common cause with their immediate social superiors, the shopkeepers. These latter, organized in their powerful and change-resistant guilds, proved to be fatal allies. Establishing what came to be recognized as a characteristic revolutionary pattern, they abandoned the moderate proletarians just as soon as the extremists were suppressed and re-established the old order more or less intact. Thus, in 1382, the Florentine oligarchy recovered power and restored the old institutions, eliminating from the city's government virtually all the hard-won influence of the lower class. Indeed, urban insurrections of this sort occurred throughout Europe and frequently attained the same startling but transitory success. Earlier, in the 1340's, a similar social upheaval had shaken the Greek city of Thessalonica. There a sailors' guild massacred about one hundred patricians and attempted to rule through a lower-class democratic government; but, as in Florence, final victory was seized by the patricians.

Nor was social disturbance limited to the cities. Reference has already been made to the French shepherds, or *Pastoureaux*, who set out in 1320 to relieve Jerusalem, but rapidly turned against the symbols of authority in the neighboring towns and then exhausted their fury attacking the Jews. In Italy, at the beginning of the century, a certain Fra Dolcino preached a doctrine which combined mystical religion with hatred for the rich and attracted a band of some 4,000 companions who terrorized the Lombard countryside from the hills around Novara and Vercelli for years. Flanders too experienced rural discontent. From 1323 until 1328, the peasants of the western maritime provinces fought against tithes and taxes in a violent civil war characterized by pillaging and destruction. Not surprisingly, the fourteenth century also saw the emergence of Robin Hood as a fully developed folk hero—the outlaw who made life miserable for the rich, but gave clear instructions to his followers to "do no husbonde harm that tilleth with his ploughe."

One major factor in the widespread rural discontent during the fourteenth century was the devastation wrought by war. Mediaeval warriors seemed to love nothing better than to loot and burn the peasants' huts and fields. In France, for example, in 1358, during the worst period of the Hundred Years' War, the peasants reacted like crazed animals in a wild outburst which came to be known as the *Jacquerie*. Although this was by far the most serious and widespread rural revolt experienced in France until the

Revolution, the nobility was able eventually to subdue the disorganized peasants. "The misery caused by
the nobles," according to one chronicler, "reached
such a pitch . . . that there was no need for the
enemy English to come to complete the destruction
of the countryside."

And the English, it might be added, were soon occupied by an uprising of their own countryside in the
Peasants' Revolt of 1381. Here, as elsewhere, the
causes were manifold but the same basic pattern could
be recognized. The rural laborers who as a result of
the Black Death had been able to alleviate their miserable condition now began to feel both the impact of
the increasing economic instability and the effect of
the new repressive statutes aimed at reducing them
once again to their pre-plague status. Having just begun to raise their heads, they were in no mood to
submit again; bitter resentment smouldered until
open revolt was finally touched off by a series of poll
taxes. The conflagration of rebellion was fanned by
primitive communists such as the renegade priest
John Ball, who preached that "things cannot go well
in England, nor ever will until everything shall be in
common . . . and all distinctions leveled." After several successful provincial uprisings, the rebellious
peasants converged on London in 1381 and, thanks
to their momentum and the indolence of the authorities, took the city. Believing that they had only to get
the ear of the king, the peasants faltered. The four-

teen-year-old Richard II bravely met them and promised to accede to their demands, but during one of the parleys the peasant leader, Wat Tyler, was struck down by the Lord Mayor of London. At once leaderless and naïvely confident of the sincerity of the King's promises, the rebels dispersed, leaving themselves vulnerable to the inevitable savage reprisals. The flames of revolt dissipated in the air like smoke.

Although the various social revolts of the fourteenth century differed in detail, they had important common traits. Most remarkable was the widespread involvement of the poor. For the first time since the fall of the Roman Empire, they began to act as an independent pressure group within the framework of society; and one distinguished historian, Christopher Dawson, even declares that "at no other time in European history has the common people asserted itself more vigorously or found more remarkable leaders." Violent as they were, these revolts of the poor were regularly frustrated at the brink of success by three circumstances. First, needless to say, the upper classes were infinitely better organized, better supplied, and, in the long run, possessed of a greater sense of common purpose. Members of the ruling classes were frequently at odds among themselves, but when their class interests were seriously threatened they always managed to lay aside their differences and act together with great vigor. Second, the poor proved unable to make lasting, broadly based alliances. The rural poor, being widely dispersed throughout fields and villages, found it difficult to meet and organize, while those in towns were as seriously divided by the diverse interests of their petty trades and crafts. Merchants were instinctively hostile to lower-class demands—the Lord Mayor of London who knocked down Wat Tyler was a fishmonger by profession. Finally, the poor had no common ideology or program. Their revolts were generally spontaneous reactions to immediate abuses; and even when they did manage to justify their actions with manifestos, these most often expressed religious and ethical egalitarianism and advocated a return to the Garden of Eden. Thus their efforts, which had seemed so near success, ended in discord, leaving them helpless before the reprisals of the frightened and vindictive rich.

The Quest for Status

The pervading sense of economic insecurity and the constant threat of violence created an obsession with social status. The land-holding nobility, having become painfully conscious of its own position, began to elaborate codes to keep the other classes in their place. Some of these took the form of sumptuary laws, which regulated the sort of clothing various classes were allowed to wear. With each class thus strictly distinguished by its dress, there could never be any doubt about a person's station. Further, existing customs of heraldry and chivalry, which determined both the degrees of noble birth and standing and their appropriate representation in coats of arms and ceremonial, were elaborated and codified. In England, courts of heraldry and chivalry were established to determine rights of bearing noble insignia and to adjudicate personal disputes between gentlemen. The illustrious Order of the Garter was founded in 1340 as a society of special social merit; and English kings began the profitable sale of royal patents granting noble status for a fee. In the fourteenth century, moreover, such class distinctions carried more than ceremonial significance. During the Hundred Years' War, for example, nobles taken prisoner in battle were spared by the rules of chivalry, while the common soldiers were massacred.

The same social distinctions were reflected in literature. Most poets wrote for a noble audience and therefore exalted the conception of "gentilesse," or proper noble bearing. Gentility is the subject of an extended disquisition by Dante in his essay known as the *Convivio* and the idea is pivotal in Geoffrey Chaucer's *Canterbury Tales*. In the latter, it was the Franklin, a character standing on the verge of nobility, who was most fascinated with the characteristics of "gentilesse." Boccaccio too identified himself with the nobility in his *Decameron* when he attacked the "sort of fellows" who when "they have but little money in their pockets are all for a gentleman's daughter" and "pretend to some coat of arms, saying

'I am of such a family, and my ancestors did so and so.' " Not surprisingly, it was in the 1350's, when Boccaccio was writing the *Decameron,* that mercantile families actually did commission agents to "find" documents attesting to the ancient and noble deeds of their ancestors. If these constant efforts to secure, define, and preserve noble titles served to aggravate the social hostilities of the age, this nearly universal obsession with status was symptomatic of vast and ominous insecurities.

Dislocation and the Vision of Death

Economic upheaval, social conflict, and natural calamity produced a pronounced streak of morbidity in the personality of the fourteenth century. One of the most popular quotations of the age was St. Augustine's admonition that "nothing is more certain than death, nothing less so than the hour of its coming." The Black Death undoubtedly contributed most to this mood by the horrifying manner in which it struck. Here and there a few doctors attempted to understand the nature and extent of the catastrophe in a scientific and rational manner, but in most cases the plague was believed to be a punishment of God, a direct manifestation of divine enmity. Acting on this assumption, Europeans could only retreat into penitence or hysteria, occasionally both, as did the flagellants. During the plague years of 1348–1349, armies of penitents marched across Europe beating one another over the back with rods and lashes. Since most people felt that these flagellants were atoning not only for their own sins but for the sins of the world, they were welcomed wherever they went, and crowds assembled to accompany the beatings with tears and groans. Indeed, only the clergy, which viewed the movement as heretical, attempted to curb the hysteria; but the movement did not disappear until the end of the plague itself.

Among the mass reactions provoked by the Black Death were the contradictory tendencies to seek escape in dissolute and riotous living and to attribute all the misfortunes of the age to divine retribution for this very immorality. "We are so corrupt, the greatest number of us are so perverse," lamented one Italian writer, "that pest, war and famine no longer astonish anyone." If Europeans were never so degenerate as moralists had charged and if many individuals did seek salvation in piety and asceticism, there is no doubt that the plague produced shocking profligacy. Dress became showy and frequently bizarre, with exaggerated plumage, long-pointed toes, and an ostentatious display of expensive jewels, in spite of the vigorous condemnations of the churchmen of the period. At the same time interest in black magic and witchcraft increased and the heresy of the Free Spirit, which justified sexual license and social immorality, found many eager converts. A similar development was the deviant movement known as the "dancers."

Its devotees, both men and women, marched or danced through the countryside in perverse imitation of the flagellants, substituting promiscuity for penitence. The candid accounts of the Free Spirit heretics and the dancers in contemporary chronicles would have been censored until a very few years ago.

The new mood also pervaded the visual arts. While works of the twelfth and thirteenth centuries had expressed hope and faith, those of the fourteenth more often stressed the morbid and the pessimistic. Among the most popular themes were the seven deadly sins and the Last Judgment, both depicted with graphic details of hellish torments and frightful beasts. The same tendencies can be seen, especially during the last half of the century, in the transformation of the Crucifixion from a subject of redemption and triumph to one of pity and terror. The Virgin, who in the high Middle Ages had radiated hope in these scenes, became increasingly somber and pathetic until she is finally seen slumping in tears at the foot of the Cross.

This obsession with the macabre increased as the century progressed. Tombstone statues frequently depicted putrefying bodies, and there are countless illustrations of death carrying off healthy young men and women. Even the literature of the century is replete with gallows humor, such as the story of an old Italian dying of the plague. Avoided by his children and friends for fear of contagion, he called his notary to add to his will the stipulation that on each anniversary of his death his heirs must leave a basket of pears for the flies. "In my sickness," he reasoned, "all my friends and relations have deserted me while only the flies have remained loyal. Thus I would not dare to ask grace from God if I did not prove thankful to them." The character of this all-pervasive mood was perhaps never better summarized than by the Greek who wrote, "Good fortune rarely smiles on us, and when it comes it withers as quickly as a flower, but this is by the will of God that we may be rightly chastened, otherwise we might get above ourselves and forget that we are mortal."

In the fourteenth century, the structure of European civilization was wracked by a series of desperate crises that inflicted deep injury on the personality of the age. Despite the morbid reactions provoked by these calamities, however, the survivors managed to muster courage and energy to contain their fears and to continue to struggle with the problems that threatened to overwhelm them.

CHAPTER II

Struggle

AT the opening of the fourteenth century, prospects for political development were poor. The great thirteenth-century institutions were showing signs of strain, and a deep economic depression was beginning to make itself felt. To these ominous developments were rapidly added fateful accidents: the sudden disappearance of men of stature, then the beginning of a series of severe famines, and finally, in mid-century, an unprecedented epidemic of the plague. It is hardly surprising that society reeled under these blows. Authority—like the economy—was weakened and fragmented. Men saw their rights and interests threatened and reacted with desperation; armed conflict became the norm rather than the exception, creating the impression that Europe was dissolving into anarchy. And yet scrutiny of the record will reveal less disintegration than might have been expected. For one thing, most participants strove to shore up traditional institutions. Even when they failed, the resulting disintegration of political order tended to be temporary and partial in England and France, although more nearly complete and lasting in Germany and Italy. Among the ruins of the old order, however, significant new departures can sometimes be discerned. When their defenses began to crumble, men resorted to vigorous improvisation. The results were bewildering in their variety and defy neat summary, let alone systematization, but some general trends can perhaps be detected.

With the breakdown of central authority men were thrown back on their own resources, which usually meant close consultation among and cooperation with their fellows of a given class and locality. Sometimes viable solutions were achieved by mutual submission to an impartial arbitrator, other times by organizing the process of consultation. In their adversity, that is, they were often not only forced to face unexpected problems but driven to attempt unprecedented solutions which—even though clearly the result of efforts to bolster the crumbling remains of old, established institutions—nevertheless occasionally suggest new, "modern" departures which lend both interest and significance to the political history of the age.

The most powerful rulers of the fourteenth century, with few exceptions, were those whose careers came to an end shortly after it began. Edward I of England, Philip IV of France, and Pope Boniface VIII, all extremely vigorous men, shared a common failing of trying to do too much too soon. By an excessive use of force and craft, they accomplished a great deal. They also made enemies of their victims and dissipated the confidence of their friends. Both Edward I and Philip IV lived to see their greatly extended royal authority threatened by aristocratic reactions, while Boniface VIII saw his unprecedented claims of papal hegemony utterly rejected. Even the luster of their very considerable achievements was eclipsed by the time these ambitious rulers died, and their subjects were left to stumble on in search of security in the gathering darkness of depression and confusion. The directions this search took can best be followed by examining the separate histories of each of the leading European powers.[1]

England—Political Chaos

Only three kings succeeded Edward I to the throne of England in the fourteenth century. Of these, two —Edward II and Richard II—were deposed for flagrant ineptitude, while the far more able and successful Edward III outlived his years of energy and terminated his reign in dotage. Taken together, their exercise of royal authority was far too weak and vacillating to dominate the turbulent forces of the period.

By the time Edward I died in 1307, his magnates

[1] Spain and Scandinavia will not be discussed in this essay. Although they constituted part of western Christendom and did interact with the major European countries, their internal histories were marked by dreary and pointless turmoil.

were in a dangerously rebellious mood. As the fighting, especially in Scotland, had become more expensive and less rewarding, his subjects had begun to
chafe with the result that, along with the crown,
Edward II also inherited the resentments provoked
by his father's unusual and unpopular methods of
raising money to finance his aggressive foreign poli-
cies. To have handled such a situation, a successor
would have needed a clear purpose, a genius for dip-
lomacy, and an iron will. Unfortunately, Edward II
was a mercurial weakling. His normal reaction to any
problem was indecision, and his will, on those rare
occasions when it became engaged, was usually mis-
directed. These flaws were compounded by eccentric
tastes and a scandalous attachment to his favorite,
Piers Gaveston. Charitable historians have been content to call Edward abnormal, while others have suggested that he was actually deranged. By neither interpretation was he fit to rule.

Edward's deficiencies were evident from the start.
At his accession he handed over his responsibilities
to Gaveston. This disreputable foreign adventurer,
by his arrogance and incompetence, promptly drove
the already restless and disaffected barons into a league
which forced Edward, in 1311, to accept new constitutional limitations on his royal authority. Still under his favorite's spell, Edward tried to evade the
commitments he had made. In response, the barons
opened civil war. Although they captured and ex-

ecuted Gaveston and forced Edward himself to sur-
render within a year, they still failed to establish a
lasting peace. By their execution of his favorite they
had driven Edward to a secret but unswerving determination to seek vengeance.

With the country thus weakened by internal strife,
the English suffered their greatest military disaster
abroad in decades. The Scots, though repeatedly defeated by Edward I, had never been thoroughly sub-
dued. Taking advantage of the respite offered by his
enemies' dissension, Robert Bruce rallied and united
his countrymen to win, at Bannockburn, in 1314, one
of the most glorious victories in Scottish history. This
stunning upset prepared the way for the revival of
the Scottish kingdom and established Bruce and his
spider in Scottish legend. It also robbed Edward II
of any prestige he may have retained. Thus even
though he did manage to defeat his barons in 1322
and repeal their reforms, his triumph was destined to
be short-lived. Within five years, his wife, Queen
Isabella, popularly known as "the she-wolf of France,"
had raised an army and taken him prisoner; and after
forcing him to abdicate, she brought his misrule to an
end by having him murdered in captivity.

England's future looked far from promising in
1327. Edward's only son was still a minor, and Isabella had consolidated her power by seizing the re-
gency. But the son was wholly different from his
father. After watching his mother abuse her power

for three years, the young Edward III overthrew her by force and, in 1330, began what was to be the longest and most popular reign of the century. As conventional as his father had been eccentric, he devoted his energies to that most respected royal occupation, warfare. He was, in fact, an able soldier, and as long as he continued to be successful on the field, he commanded the loyalties and affections of his people.

Edward inaugurated his military career most auspiciously by restoring English military prestige at the expense of the Scots. Taking advantage of Scotland's weakness after the death of Robert Bruce in 1329 to reopen hostilities, Edward won a victory at Halidon Hill in 1333 which established him in the hearts of his countrymen and gave him the necessary support to embark on a collision course with France. But in this new venture success was neither swift nor easy. Instead, his aggressive policy was to drag on in a ruinous conflict with the French which has come to be known as the Hundred Years' War. As a result of his initial failure to win more swift successes, Edward's authority in England was undermined; and he was only able to surmount a threatened baronial rebellion, in 1340–1341, by politic maneuvering, determined resistance, and sweeping concessions. Then finally, in 1346 and 1356, respectively, the extraordinary victories of Crécy and Poitiers completely re-established his position with his restive subjects by laying all

France open to their aggressive energies and rapacious ambitions. Now, celebrated as a hero, Edward reigned peacefully over a tranquil and prosperous England until, at the end of his long reign, his advancing senility and a lull in the French war combined to provoke once again the ever-incipient baronial unrest.

Having ruled for fifty years, Edward III had outlived his eldest son—the chivalric "Black Prince"—and left his throne to his grandson the young Richard II. In character and career almost a reprise of his great-grandfather Edward II, this prince was, if anything, even more unusual. He was, for example, a patron of the arts, and he seems to have detested war out of moral principle, two attributes as little appreciated as they were unexpected in a mediaeval monarch. And although he possessed great personal charm, he was at once as vain and frivolous, as vindictive and deceitful, as Edward II. Obsessively suspicious and headstrong, he resented the inevitable attempts to limit his authority by constitutional restrictions. Some historians have seen in this trait a foreshadowing of modern theories of absolutism; but if Richard did nurture any such ideas of untrammeled rule, he was peculiarly unsuited to the task of imposing them on his rebellious nobles. His reign was marked by violent fits of rage and the equally violent reactions of his turbulent and disaffected subjects, just as his place in history would seem to have been determined by the

tragic flaws of character which have been so widely
exploited by romantic biographers, speculative psy-
chologists, and Shakespeare.

Since Richard had been only ten when he succeeded to the throne in 1377, the royal authority was
confided to an aristocratic council. Four years later,
during the peasant rebellion of 1381, the boy king
saved the day for his guardians by a remarkable display of personal courage; and by the time he was
eighteen he was ready to make a bid for independence
from his tenacious regents. Unsuccessful, mainly because he had espoused the unpopular cause of peace
with France, he was not able to free himself from
baronial control until 1389. Then, like Edward II, he
harbored bitter resentment against those who had attempted to limit or usurp his power. Hiding his intentions behind a deceptive facade of moderate government for eight long years, he finally struck in
1397. With no hint of warning, he suddenly charged
his old enemies with treason and had them arrested,
tried, and executed in swift succession. When a parliament, packed for the purpose, then granted him
revenues for life, he apparently had created the base
for purely arbitrary rule. But Richard had moved too
fast and he had made a fatal error. Overestimating
his strength, he decided on a campaign in Ireland.
As soon as he had left England, however, the country
rose in revolt. When he returned to deal with the
insurrection, he was arrested by his own cousin

Henry of Lancaster, deposed, and secretly put to death. Thus, a century-long struggle between crown and barons played itself to a fitting end with the murder of a headstrong king.

England—Constitutional Progress

The longer and more bitterly the king contended with his barons, the more urgent and apparent became the need for order and continuity in the central government. But if the very confusion of the period contributed to this need, it also tended to obscure the origins of important new stabilizing institutions.

The fundamental organ of administration in England had been the royal council or *curia regis*.[2] Originally an unspecialized and undifferentiated body of magnates serving as royal advisers, the council was, by the fourteenth century, becoming a body of trained administrative servants of the crown. The barons, however, reluctant to abandon what they considered their right to participate in making royal policy, never ceased their efforts to dominate the council. But even though they frequently gained the upper hand, they were never able to control the actual government for long.

Lacking the experience, the temperament, and the capacity to handle complicated and tiresome administrative business, they invariably left, or returned, such work to the newly trained experts. These, in

[2] See Sidney Painter, *The Rise of the Feudal Monarchies* (Ithaca, N.Y., 1951), pp. 76–79.

turn, tended to find the kings personally more con-
genial than the unruly barons and the concept of
monarchy more adaptable to their purposes than that
of feudal independence. In this situation the kings
were able, by vigilant resistance to all baronial encroachments, to retain at least nominal control of the
council throughout the century. Nor had the long
struggle been in vain, since it had served to define
more sharply the specific functions of central government and to establish irrevocably the need for administrative specialists. In fact, the professional bu-
reaucracy had become so efficient in its methods and
so firmly entrenched in its position that no major
changes in its structure or procedures were needed
for another hundred years.

The best known branch of the royal council was
Parliament. In simplest terms it was the largest open
meeting of the council, but its functions and membership had been only vaguely defined until the fourteenth century. Then, as the work of the council became more and more technical, Parliament came to
be used less and less for general bureaucratic business.
Instead it established its own special preserves and
prerogatives, particularly in the areas of justice, legislation, and taxation. As the full meeting of the royal
council, Parliament was accepted as the highest court
of the realm. In this capacity it heard special cases and
occasionally tried royal officials in the judicial process
of impeachment. It was also coming to be recognized

as a legislative body, a function which carried implications of the utmost importance for the future. Or-
dinances decreed by the king had been accepted as
binding for his lifetime. During the thirteenth and
fourteenth centuries, however, it was gradually
agreed that statutes passed by king and Parliament
together would have the force of permanent law.
And finally, by exercising the authority to levy taxes,
Parliament had laid the cornerstone of its power. As
early as 1297, Edward I had agreed to impose general
taxation only with the consent of "the community of
the realm." By the early fourteenth century, this
term was accepted to mean the consent of Parliament
and the principle was clarified and reinforced in the
concessions made by Edward III during the crisis of
1340. With the right of control over the royal purse
strings firmly established, if not vigorously exploited,
in the fourteenth century, Parliament had captured a
strategic position from which it was destined to serve
as one of England's most important bulwarks against
the threat of royal absolutism.

The implications of these intrinsic powers made it
important to regulate the membership of Parliament.
From time to time, apparently to serve his own interests, Edward I had summoned representatives of
the counties and towns to Parliament. Gradually they
were called more and more often until it would
hardly have occurred to anyone to do without them.
At what point they began to attend regularly and of

their own right, however, would be as difficult to date precisely as most other points of transition in the development of the English constitution. All we know for certain is that town and county representatives had not been essential to the functioning of Parliament at the beginning of the fourteenth century and had become the House of Commons by the end. At the same time, those great magnates who failed to entrench themselves in the inner council of the king began to meet in what was to become the House of Lords. This regular representation of the Commons and the division of Parliament into two separate houses were to become the most enduring and most important hallmarks of the English constitution.

The development of Parliament continued uninterrupted through the century. The crown and magnates both believed they could use it to their own ends, and both therefore tried to increase its powers. Thus, in their efforts to dominate Edward II, the barons tried to subject him to parliamentary control, while he, in turn, tried to strengthen Parliament as an institutional defense against their encroachments. In spite of such impressive gains, however, Parliament remained a supplementary branch of government. Day-to-day administration was handled by the royal council, and both king and country could still have circumvented the Parliament entirely. The reason they did not do so may be attributed in part, perhaps, to the English respect for precedent. Once Parliament was established it was accepted and thereby given the opportunity to develop its potential.

The troubled history of the century fostered the growth of one more characteristic English institution —the office of justice of the peace. The traditional representative of the crown in local affairs had been the sheriff. These royal officers, once both popular and efficient, had been given more and more duties until they had begun to lose both their effectiveness and their popularity. The countryside's hatred for the evil sheriff in *Robin Hood*, for example, represented an attitude which had become widespread well before the fourteenth century. To check the abuses of this office and at the same time to implement the extensive social legislation drawn up after the Black Death, the crown resorted increasingly to the new local officers.

These justices of the peace, as they were called, had important advantages over the sheriff for both king and country. First they came from the ranks of the local gentry, or landowners, which meant that they were known and respected by those they served as well as loyal and responsive to the king who had appointed them. Further, many had represented their counties in Parliament, from which the sheriffs were excluded, and therefore had acquired experience in legal and fiscal matters which was as useful as it was unusual. And finally, from the point of view of the crown, always concerned with keeping the royal budget within limits, the fact that they served without salary was probably not the least of their attractions. In "Quarter Sessions"—so called because they were held four times a year—the justices not only presided over the local courts but also transacted a great amount of administrative business. And if in times of anarchy, when the royal power was being successfully challenged, they were no match for the local barons, under strong kings the justices demonstrated the capacity of local self-government to cooperate effectively with royal authority.

France—the Hundred Years' War

At the beginning of the fourteenth century, the prestige of the French monarchy had no equal in all Europe. The saintly Louis IX had perfected the royal constitution which he had inherited from his Capetian predecessors; and under his benign rule the country had prospered as never before. Later his grandson Philip IV enlarged the royal territory abroad at the expense of Germany, increased French power by making the pope his client, and vastly extended the crown's authority within the realm. Known to posterity as "the Fair," Philip was also known to his contemporaries as "the Owl—the handsomest of birds which is worth absolutely nothing. . . ." This characterization of a king who apparently accomplished so much would seem to refer to an important development within the monarchical institution. For some time in France, as in England, the king's business had been increasingly entrusted to, or pre-empted by, professional bureaucrats who in turn were increasingly drawn from the legal profession. For the first time, in the reign of Philip, these royal legists began to play not only an important but a public, and possibly even an independent, role in governing the kingdom. Indeed the question seems to have been raised whether Philip was really more than a handsome figurehead behind which his administrators worked to serve and develop the institution, if not the personification, of the monarchy; but it is a question to which modern historians have no final answer.

Philip and his ministers did much for France, but their methods were all too often unsavory and not in keeping with the high-minded policy of Philip's saintly grandfather. Like his contemporary Edward I of England, Philip waged expensive wars which drove him to devious means of raising money. Illustrative is his treatment of the Templars, a military order originally founded in the twelfth century after the conquest of Palestine to protect pilgrims and defend the Kingdom of Jerusalem. In the course of time, however, they had acquired great wealth, which they used to provide and transfer credit for pilgrims and crusaders. When the Christian outposts in the Holy Land were lost, the Templars, of necessity, returned to Europe, where they put their financial capital and skills at the service of the king of France. Once they had become his principal bankers, however, they inevitably invited the traditional fate of royal moneylenders. Stripped of their religious purpose and military prestige, they were as vulnerable as they were tempting, and in 1307 one of the king's most unscrupulous lawyers manufactured a battery of charges against the order, including heresy and homosexuality. All the Templars in France were rapidly arrested and many, under ruthless interrogation, confessed. With this evidence Philip bullied the Pope into action, and although the affair dragged on for years, the order of the Templars was finally suppressed by a general council of the Church in 1312. Ironically, however, their property was given to another military order, the Hospitalers; and Philip was only able to seize the amount he claimed the Templars owed him. The largest part of their wealth, which had been his real objective, eluded his grasp.

In other efforts he was more successful. He expelled the Jews from the realm and, following well-established royal precedent, confiscated all their remaining goods. He also appropriated the holdings of the Italian bankers in France, who by this time were far wealthier than the Jews. Further, he manipulated the currency to royal advantage and managed to collect taxes that none of his predecessors had been able to impose. Still, government had become more costly and Philip's wars were so expensive that he was always in need of new funds. When he died in 1314, monarchical institutions were well developed and

France was the envy of her neighbors. But Philip's subjects were disgruntled, tired of the financial strain, and suspicious of the monarchy.

Feudal and provincial reaction followed. In 1315, one year after Philip's death and exactly a century after the promulgation of the Magna Carta in England, Louis X was obliged to grant a series of charters to his rebellious provincial nobles. Unlike the famous English model, however, these charters contained little that could be construed as constructive constitutional limitation of royal power. The very fact that the barons demanded a series of provincial charters instead of a charter for the entire kingdom suggests the highly particular, not to say selfish, nature of their demands and explains the ultimate weakness of their opposition. Unable to unite in a common cause, the French barons could never agree on a viable alternative to monarchical rule and could, therefore, rarely impose their will on their sovereign, no matter how weak or unpopular he might be. Furthermore, in the confusion created by the economic depression and natural calamities of the fourteenth century, the security offered by even oppressive monarchical rule had a seductive appeal in France.

Louis X, known as "the Stubborn," died in 1316, to be succeeded in rapid succession by his two brothers. When the second died in 1328, the Capetian line, which had succeeded from father to son for over three hundred years, came to an end, leaving the

French for the first time in centuries facing a disputed succession. By the most common feudal usage the crown would have passed to the daughter of Philip the Fair or at least through her to her male progeny. But her son was none other than the young Edward III of England. Confronted with the prospect of an English king mounting the French throne, the royal lawyers announced that the crown should not descend to, or through, a woman and gave the succession to the son of Philip's brother, thereby creating the new Valois dynasty. Later, when controversy raged over this decision, the lawyers argued that it was based on an ancient Frankish custom which they termed the "Salic Law." Thus they established a principle that lasted as long as the French monarchy and that entailed a series of serious consequences.

If at first the establishment of a new dynasty appeared a reasonable solution of the problem, that impression was quickly dispelled by Philip VI, who proved to be a quixotic fool. Edward, who could easily claim he had been excluded from his rightful succession to the crown of France, saw an irresistible temptation in the evident frivolity of his successful rival. When Philip intervened brutally in a civil struggle in Flanders, where English interests and influence were dominant, Edward seized the opportunity for which he had been waiting by declaring himself king of France; Philip responded by declaring Edward's French fiefs forfeited. With these actions both kings contributed significantly to the complicated causes which embroiled France in the disastrous Hundred Years' War.

Even though it is unlikely that Edward really expected to occupy the French throne, his claim provided him with both a convenient pretext and an excellent lever for extracting concessions from his rival. The contention between them quickly found a focus in fiefs, notably Saintonge and the Bordelais, which Edward held directly from the French crown. This extremely rich wine-producing region had been in English hands since the twelfth century and its trade with London was an important source of income. Not surprisingly, the English intended to retain this last and most valuable part of their ancient Duchy of Gascony no matter what the cost. The French crown lawyers, on the other hand, had come to regard as anachronistic all feudal relationships that were not of advantage to the king. By the beginning of the fourteenth century, therefore, they were very much inclined to consider Edward's fiefs an integral part of the French realm. As officers of the French crown they expected to establish their royal authority in Gascony just as they were doing throughout the rest of the kingdom, even if that should require the expulsion of the English. And the English, for their part, were quite as determined to eliminate all royal hindrances in order to extend their feudal title to outright possession and control of the lucrative fief.

Armed conflict over this area had already broken out briefly during the reigns of Edward I and Philip the Fair, and tense relations had persisted ever since.

Actually, however, it was not in Gascony but Flanders that the French and English first came to serious blows. Economically, Flanders was one of the most advanced and prosperous regions of Europe. Its very prosperity, however, produced special problems both at home and abroad. The unusual business methods which had evolved with, and contributed to, the prosperity of the towns of the region made intolerable the traditional feudal relations either with the local aristocracy or the royal suzerain, the king of France. With wealth on such an unprecedented scale apparently within their grasp, the French kings were bound to resist with all their might any efforts the Flemish towns might make to gain their independence. To this end the kings regularly tried to bolster their own position and weaken that of the towns by supporting the latter's traditional enemies, the rural aristocrats. The English, who by this time were deeply involved in the Flemish wool trade, did their utmost to defend the towns and reduce the influence of the French. It was from this confused struggle that the Hundred Years' War finally erupted in 1337.

The major battles of the war were a series of disasters for the French. From experience gained fighting the Welsh and Scots, the English had discovered the value of the longbow and had developed tactics which exploited its advantages. The French, who still relied on the traditional cavalry charge and chivalric heroism, were picked off with deadly efficiency by the English bowmen. Nor were the French able to adopt or counter this new technique. It has long been thought that social prejudice against common soldiers prevented them from developing an infantry of their own, but the problem was much more complex. Mastery of the bow demanded both great skill and great strength and therefore, much like mastery of the art of fighting on horseback, required constant practice, effectively placing it beyond the capacities of ordinary peasants. The French, thus, had little to put against the new English tactics except courage. As a result, when the two armies met directly on the field, the numerically inferior English invariably prevailed and, at Crécy in 1346 and Poitiers ten years later, crushed the French in two of the most famous battles of the Middle Ages.

The French king, John the Good, who had succeeded Philip VI in 1350, was taken prisoner in the total defeat at Poitiers and carried off to England. France was left in chaos. As a contemporary chronicler noted, "Thenceforward infinite harm, misfortune, and danger befell the French people for lack of good government and adequate defense." It was in this difficult period, however, that John's son, Charles, was able to rally the people in the French countryside to defend themselves against the marauding English. He then obtained a temporary respite by signing the Treaty of Brétigny in 1360, which gave Edward III outright possession of Gascony in the south and Calais and Ponthieu in the north in return for renunciation of his claim to the French throne. John the Good was freed on the promise of an enormous ransom, but when it became clear the French could never raise it, John gallantly returned to England, where he died in 1364.

Awed by their own glittering triumphs in the field, the English were convinced that they could completely conquer France. But the fact was they could not. Lacking the manpower to occupy and garrison so large a country, they could never fully subdue French opposition. Yet the war dragged on because the English king needed the prestige of victories, and his barons lusted for the profits of plunder. Like Falstaff's ragtag comrades, they were responsive to the cry:

> Let us to France; like horse-leeches my boys,
> To suck, to suck, the very blood to suck.

Under the resourceful leadership of Charles V, who formally succeeded his father in 1364, the French began to defend themselves effectively when the English broke the tenuous truce and resumed hostilities. In the wily Breton Bertrand du Guesclin, Charles found a military commander of unusual talent. Taking a leaf from the book of the famous Ro-

man commander Fabius, du Guesclin refused to
offer battle. Instead he wore the English down by
harassing them with petty raids, seizing and holding
castles, and organizing local resistance. The war splut-
tered on into the fifteenth century, but the English,
thoroughly exhausted by these tactics, lost both their
initiative and almost all their newly acquired lands.
With the English held at bay, the French enjoyed a
period of respite and convalescence. Charles, now
known as "the Wise," was even able to revive the
prestige and authority of the monarchy both at home
and abroad. His premature death in 1380 was a dou-
ble calamity, however, because it deprived the country of his great services and left it to the mismanage-
ment of Charles VI. This poor son of an able father
soon gave evidence of insanity, offering the English
an open invitation to launch a fresh invasion. Once
again English arms were to be crowned with spectacular success.

The internal political development which took
place in France during, and in part because of, the
struggle with the English offers a highly significant
contrast to what was happening across the channel.
Following the defeat at Crécy, a meeting of the Estates-General refused to grant further war levies and
demanded fiscal reforms. By this time, the Estates
that Philip IV had summoned from the entire realm
had taken to meeting in two separate sections: one
north of the Loire River representing the area called

Langue d'Oil and the other in the south, or *Langue d'Oc*.[3] These names derived from the regional accents with which the inhabitants spoke French, and southern France is still occasionally referred to as Languedoc. In 1355, however, the Estates of both north and south joined in a rare display of coordinated action to force John to grant important concessions. He did commit himself to consulting the Estates before making any new financial levies; but almost immediately he began to organize an opposition which Charles was able to maintain when he became regent following his father's capture at Poitiers. When need of funds forced Charles to call the Estates in 1357, he was confronted with an extended set of demands, embodied in a Great Ordinance, obviously intended to give the Estates the sort of financial control that the Parliament was beginning to assume in England. Although he found it expedient to acquiesce at the time, the success of the Estates was short-lived. Not only did they relapse into their old division, but their most important leader, Etienne Marcel, made a fatal error. Because of the general chaos caused by the war and the consequent exactions and depredations of both the royal army and the free mercenary companies, the peasants had risen in a violent revolt called the *Jacquerie*. In an attempt to gain popular support for the Estates against the king, Marcel, who was the

[3] See Painter, *Feudal Monarchies*, pp. 40, 41.

richest merchant of Paris, began intriguing with the peasant leaders. This unprecedented step immediately and completely alienated the nobility, with the consequence that Marcel was murdered and Charles was able not only to return to Paris but also to re-establish the monarchy's authority throughout the country.

There are many reasons why the history of the Estates is so strikingly different from that of Parliament. The fact that the Estates were normally called only in major crises made them appear more revolutionary than constitutional and thus alienated the large majority of their potential supporters. Furthermore, the French were more deeply divided than the English not only by class but also by local loyalties. Both the use of free farmers, or yeomen, in the army and the fact that the lesser nobles or knights sat as county representatives alongside the burgesses in the House of Commons are cited as examples of social integration in England that could not be matched in France. There the peasants were rigorously excluded from any but servile occupations and the townspeople were considered social inferiors and political rivals by the nobles. To this social prejudice must be added the fact that provincial loyalties were often stronger than those to the monarchy and that the interests of the northern and southern halves of the country were frequently quite disparate. As a result, the establishment of a unified constitutional opposition was extremely difficult; and the very failure of the Estates, at least by contrast, served to enhance the prestige of the crown.

This prestige, unequaled in Europe, was due to a number of factors. Typical of these was the elaborate coronation ceremony at Reims in which the king was anointed with a holy unction which, it was widely believed, had been brought down from heaven by the Holy Spirit in the form of a dove and which gave the king miraculous powers including the ability to cure the scrofula by a touch of his hand. Another very different but no less important factor was the work of the vigorous and resourceful propagandists who served the later Capetians and who in the reign of Philip the Fair not only called the French crown "the arbitrator of the truth" but actually claimed its hegemony over Europe. These lofty pretensions were somewhat tarnished by Philip's chicanery; and none of his immediate successors was sufficiently able or glamorous to reimpose the respect previously enjoyed by the monarchy. Not until Charles V did a French king restore the damage suffered by the crown. Thanks to the services of sagacious advisers and gifted craftsmen as well as to the display of wealth and power, he made his court an early model for taste, opulence, and authority of the sort Versailles was to become in later centuries. Moreover, unable to compete with his rival Edward III as a dashing military figure, Charles successfully propagated the notion that the king need not lead his troops into battle. It was actually, counted to his credit that he had reconquered "in the chamber" everything that his predecessors had lost "on the field." In sum, this new increase of prestige lent the French monarchy authority in European affairs and later helped tide it over difficult times when the head that wore the crown lacked competence.

Germany—the View toward the East

If life in Germany during the fourteenth century was no less chaotic than in England and France, that was the only important common experience the Empire shared with the western monarchies, and even in this there was the important difference that chaos was nothing new in Germany. While the royal powers were being consolidated in England and France, those of the emperors were being dissipated in the endless struggles of the twelfth and thirteenth centuries. By the beginning of the fourteenth, the western boundaries of the Empire were being threatened by the French and the vestigial authority of the emperor was being challenged in Germany by the claims of the popes and the machinations of the princes. Thus England and France entered the crisis of the fourteenth century with vigorous monarchical institutions, but the Empire seemed on the verge of dissolution and its supporters had to cast about desperately for new expedients to keep it functioning at all. In the confusion of the age it is not surprising that these efforts seemed to have little direction and less success, yet in the long run they established a new orientation that was to influence German development down to the end of World War II.

At the beginning of the fourteenth century, Albert of Hapsburg had made a valiant effort to curb the burgeoning power of the princes, but in 1308 he was murdered by his nephew. This treacherous act opened the gates to the full tide of reaction. Since the emperors had never been able to establish the principle of hereditary succession, the great princes had no difficulty, in this critical juncture, in skipping over Albert's Hapsburg heir and electing an obscure count from the western borderland, Henry of Luxembourg. His chief attraction was his utter insignificance; but he was intelligent enough to recognize that Albert's failure was the direct result of his opposition to the princes. A strange blend of realist and romantic, Henry VII, as he was called, made no effort to follow his predecessor's vigorous but futile policy. Rather than attempt to defend the hollow pretensions of the imperial title, he set out to build a solid base of power beyond the reach of the jealous princes by acquiring the crown of Bohemia for his family. But his realistic approach to German affairs gave way to tragic romanticism where Italy was concerned. The German emperors had always claimed dominion over Italy and in the twelfth and thirteenth centuries had come

close to making good their claim. In the early fourteenth century, however, Henry's journey to Italy
was hopelessly ill conceived. The very fact that he
was welcomed at first as a savior by Dante and the
remnants of the old imperial party should have
warned him that he was engaged in an anachronistic
misadventure. Henry, however, had himself crowned
in Rome in 1311 at the cost of becoming inextricably
mired in the morass of Italian politics. He floundered
on until his army, exhausted by sieges and wasted by
disease, disintegrated around him. In 1313 he himself
was poisoned, it was said, by a priest who mixed a
deadly brew in the chalice of the Eucharist. Such
was the end of the last mediaeval German emperor
who attempted to exercise dominion over Italy.

The election of his successor was contested in over
thirty years of civil war. The strongest candidate,
Louis of Bavaria, defeated his Hapsburg rival on the
battlefield, but he was never able to overcome the
opposition of the Pope either by military action or by
abject submission. The contest spread into Germany
in the form of a protracted armed struggle between
Louis and the Pope's German supporters which not
only exhausted the country but squandered any remaining prestige of the imperial title. In the end, the
electors abandoned Louis in favor of Charles of Bohemia, the grandson of Henry VII.

Having learned from Louis' failure that no emperor could withstand the combined onslaught of

both the princes and the pope, Charles decided to seek a new base of power. In 1356, he sealed an alliance with the princes by issuing the Golden Bull, which eliminated the claims of the pope in Germany.

By giving full control over the imperial succession to the prince-electors, the Golden Bull not only denied the pope's claim to rights in the election but effectively eliminated his influence in the Empire. It also granted the electoral princes full sovereignty in their own principalities, a precedent which once established for these magnates would inevitably be used by lesser princes to claim and establish similar powers. To eliminate papal influence from Germany, Charles had abandoned all hope of restoring an effective imperial authority and that of his successors. The solid position he had created for himself and his family in Bohemia did nothing for Germany as a whole. Indeed he was called "the father of Bohemia and the stepfather of Germany," and his worthless son, the famous drunkard Wenceslas, was deposed by the electors in 1400.

This decline of imperial power tended, among other things, to turn German interests from west to east. Taking advantage of their neighbor's weakness, the French probed the entire length of the German border for possible territorial acquisitions, while in the southwest the Swiss seized the same opportunity to constitute an autonomous confederation, making the fourteenth the most glorious century in their history.

Beginning with the fabled exploits of William Tell and the dramatic victory of Morgarten, they succeeded not only in winning their independence but in establishing their infantry as the most formidable troops on the continent. The more vigorous German dynasties sought compensation for these losses in the west by consolidating their power in the east. The Hapsburgs and the Luxembourgers, for example, had begun as petty western landholders, but both switched their attention to the east during the fourteenth century and successfully installed their dynasties in Austria and Bohemia respectively.

Equally significant was the conquest, and consolidation, of Prussia by the Teutonic Knights. A quasi-religious military order left unemployed by the end of the Crusades, the Knights had transferred their base to Prussia and from there attempted to extend their hegemony into Lithuania. Here their initial successes roused the Slavs to desperate resistance. The Poles, who had united with the Lithuanians by a royal marriage in 1386, were finally able in 1410 to overwhelm the Teutonic Knights in the now legendary battle of Tannenberg. But if this stunning defeat announced the decline and gradual disintegration of the famous military order, it did not presage any weakening of German control in Prussia, where the Hohenzollerns were to establish a family stronghold which they would eventually turn into the nucleus of a new German empire.

If the decline of imperial authority should be given credit for diverting German interest and energy from west to east, it must also be held responsible for the calamitous and progressive decentralization of German government. The great princely families had immediately attempted to seize the powers and prerogatives abandoned by the emperors, and several, notably the Hapsburgs, the Luxembourgers, and later the Hohenzollerns, were able to carve extensive independent dominions from the old imperial body. Others, however, fell victims, in their turn, to the same decentralizing tendencies. Lesser lords began to stake their claims to independent jurisdiction within their smaller political units. Frequently the process of fragmentation was continued to its logical conclusion in the minute holdings of independent knights, turning the map of Germany into a jigsaw puzzle. The local populations, with their attention concentrated in petty courts and miniature armies, lost all sense of German identity. The consequences of this dissipation of energies in petty place-seeking and miniscule wars were to paralyze the country for centuries.

In the midst of this general disintegration, and in part because of it, the fourteenth century became the golden age of German cities. Forced by circumstances to defend and govern themselves, they frequently gained their independence, and many even prospered economically while depression was ravaging the rest of Europe. Left thus to their own considerable re-

sources, they became great innovators in the art of
government. Not only did they develop administrative techniques, they experimented with such revolutionary community services as paved streets, fire
protection, and public health. Indeed, according to
one authority, "in Germany the mediaeval city was
the forerunner of the modern state."

Given the all but total chaos of the period, these
were not trivial achievements; and if the old social-
political structure was severely damaged by the collapse of the empire, the very shock of the disaster
provoked constructive reactions in some segments of
the community.

The Papacy and Italy—the Church Loses Its Leadership

Shortly after his triumphant year of jubilee, as we
have seen, Boniface VIII challenged the kings of
England and France by the bold assertion that he was
Christ's regent on earth and that consequently all
temporal authority emanated from him. If the cynical
brutality of Philip's response rallied Italian sentiments
to the Pope's defense, it also broke his spirit and contributed to his death. With no one left to dispute
his authority, Philip was free to dominate the papacy
so completely and so openly that in 1308 an observer
noted that "the King of France is pope and emperor."

To escape the vicissitudes of Italian politics and
seek the protective mantle of the king of France, the

next popes sought refuge in Avignon. Although lo-
cated in a papal enclave and nominally independent of
French suzerainty, this city-state was really in the
heart of southeastern France and under French influence. Not the least of its advantages, in the eyes of
its new residents, was its setting and its climate, both
far pleasanter than those of mediaeval Rome; and the
papal court rapidly acquired a disturbing reputation
for worldly ease and comforts. In this soil, justly
famous for its wine, the old prestige of the papacy
failed to take new root. Instead, the popes became
enmeshed in French politics, thus squandering the
popularity and support they could have drawn from
those repelled by the ruthless or incapable rulers of
England and France and at the same time discrediting
themselves by this association. The so-called Babylonian Captivity of the papacy had begun.

In addition to the new difficulties they had in-
curred by their move to Avignon, the popes had still
to contend with the great dilemma of the mediaeval
Church which they had brought with them from
Rome: the necessity, on the one hand, of a clerical
hierarchy to implement the spiritual mission of the
church, and the inevitability, on the other, of this
organization's involving them in bitter conflict with
the secular bureaucracies. As this inescapable contest
progressed, it so engrossed the attention of some
popes that many observers came to fear that the
papacy had lost sight of the primary goals of the

Church. When Boniface VIII embarked on his test of strength with the kings of England and France, he found that he could no longer count on popular support, as his predecessors often had, among the subjects of his opponents.

The obvious lesson of Boniface's tragic failure, however, was wasted on his successors. Brilliant fiscal administrators, they collected fees, taxes, and fines with such efficiency, and managed their treasury so shrewdly, that they set the papacy on the road to solvency. They also resumed the papal policy of meddling in German affairs, with some limited success against Louis of Bavaria, but at the cost of becoming generally regarded as greedy and worldly puppets. The resulting loss of spiritual prestige which the popes suffered proved to have serious consequences for the Church. Even if the men of the fourteenth century were forced by the multiple disorders of their age to concern themselves largely with mundane and even sordid problems, they were by instinct and intent no less religious than their predecessors. Already frustrated by the corruption of the times, their faith was further outraged by the shocking spectacle of the worldly popes in Avignon. Sheer disgust turned many from the Church and drove some to seek consolation in mysticism and heresy. Even the popes of Avignon recognized the threat to their position implicit in such a trend and attempted to react. But their lack of concern with serious spiritual reform was too fundamental to be successfully dissimulated and served in the end not only to defeat their efforts but to enhance the prestige of their critics.

The papacy paid dearly in public esteem, for example, for the attacks on those followers of Saint Francis known as the Spiritual Franciscans. In 1318, four extremists were burned at the stake for insisting, despite a papal ruling to the contrary, on the maintenance of absolute poverty within the Franciscan Order. Later, in 1322, the Pope drove even the moderate Franciscan general into rebellion by declaring heretical the opinion that Christ and His Apostles had held no property of their own. The fact that the Pope was also notoriously jealous of the financial position of the papacy did nothing to mitigate the public outrage. Pious Christians were left to ponder what had happened to the pristine motives of the apostolic church in the hands of such successors.

In Italy, during the absence of the popes, the customary internecine strife grew even worse. After the ignominious failure of Henry VII, all hope that stability might be imposed by German intervention had to be abandoned. Only the southern portion of the peninsula was united by a monarchy—the Kingdom of Naples—but this area was sinking into the poverty and lawlessness which has characterized it in modern times. Elsewhere, the cities of the north, blessed by greater wealth, were entering what is often called "the Age of the Despots." Having established their independence from the German Empire in the twelfth and thirteenth centuries, most of them had set up autonomous governments known as *communes* and regulated by republican principles. Increasing wealth, however, exacerbated the inevitable internal tensions. New classes that made their living from the growing trade and industry refused to accept the continued domination of the older landed classes, provoking bitter and inconclusive struggles which usually proved nothing except that neither class could permanently overcome the other. This standard impasse tended to produce a standard compromise— a strong man would be invited to impose arbitrary but impartial peace. And, once established, such strong men seldom relinquished power. Without too much trouble they were able to annul the republican constitutions and install their heirs as hereditary rulers.

This general pattern can be observed in the history of most of the cities of northern Italy. Most important was Milan. There the Visconti family established a hereditary despotism so strong that in the years around 1400 only the death of its greatest duke prevented it from conquering all of northern Italy. The major exception to the pattern was Venice. This commercial city, anchored on the Adriatic coast, had too little mainland territory to support a powerful landed class, a lack which obviated the social strife that shook her Italian neighbors and left her great shipping magnates unchallenged in their control of the oligarchic republic. Florence too was something of an exception to the pattern of Milan, but to a lesser extent. When the characteristic struggle between classes erupted, the Florentines reacted vigorously and appeared to have saved their republic, but their success was more apparent than real. Operating behind the carefully preserved traditional constitution and wearing the thin disguise of conventional titles, the crafty family known as the Medici had, by the fifteenth century, seized and maintained the same powers as those enjoyed by the other despots of the age. In sum, the rise of despotism in northern Italy helped to pave the way for the growth of small territorial states that made up in wealth and culture what they lacked in size. Some Italian historians still look back with nostalgia to the apogee of this development in the fifteenth century; but it is worth remembering that the achievements of the period had been won by long and bloody struggles.

Between the decaying southern kingdom and the rising northern cities, the area around Rome lay in chaos. With the popes in Avignon, the once-great city was abandoned to the violence of its unruly citizens, rapacious barons, and foreign mercenaries. On these, none succeeded in imposing enduring stability. In a brief interlude, however, control of the anarchic Eternal City was temporarily seized by a

native upstart, a vain romantic dreamer named Cola
di Rienzi. In contrast to the cynical foreign mercenaries, he loved Rome and sensed that, in the absence of the discredited papacy, Italy needed a new
unifying symbol of authority. To fill the void, he
tried to revive Italian pride in the ancient grandeur
of the city and its classic republican constitution.
His first efforts met with considerable success. His
highly infectious enthusiasm captured the imagination
and support of many, including the poet Petrarch,
and swept him, in 1347, to power as "Tribune of the
People." Instead of leading him on to further triumphs, these successes incited him to such outra-
geouly pompous pretensions that he was soon driven
into exile. Undaunted, he returned in 1354, only to
be slaughtered at the Capitol in the closest approxima-
tion to a revival of ancient Roman traditions that he
had been able to evoke. Politically, his attempt was
an anachronistic failure. The grandeur of his vision
may have given important impetus to that Italian
interest in the classical past which was to have such
dazzling influence in the next century, but today his
memory survives principally in the title of one of
Wagner's most immature operas.

Even after years in Avignon, the popes never fully
divested themselves of all responsibility for Rome and
finally they recognized that their return to Italy was
imperative. In the meantime, many cities within the
Papal States had been seized by despots who were

ready to defend their new holdings by force. As a result, the papacy felt it necessary, in 1353, to send the skillful diplomat and warrior Cardinal Albornoz to Italy to reimpose papal sovereignty by negotiation if possible or by the sword if necessary. After several years he achieved a partial and tenuous success. In 1367, Pope Urban V finally set out for Rome, but within three years he had beaten a retreat to Avignon, in complete despair of imposing his authority on the Italian factions. In 1376, his successor, Gregory XI, made another but futile attempt. He too would have returned to France if he had not died in 1378.

At this point, the papacy suffered its greatest disaster. While still in Rome, the cardinals hastily elevated to the chair of Peter an unusually highhanded Italian, Urban VI. Immediately ruing their choice, however, they declared his election uncanonical and elected a Frenchman, Clement VII, in his stead. Urban VI, totally rejecting his deposition, entrenched himself at Rome, and Clement VII retreated to Avignon to establish a rival papal court. The impasse was complete; and the shame of the Babylonian Captivity gave way to the scandal of the Great Schism.

Christendom had not experienced anything so degrading since the tenth century. The rival popes occupied themselves with mutual recriminations and abuse of a particularly sordid and vicious nature. By the time Urban died, his cardinals were so deeply implicated in the struggle that they sacrificed the opportunity for reconciliation to their selfish interests. Instead of seeking a compromise with Clement, they elected one of their number to succeed Urban and perpetuated the Schism. Their Avignonese opponents followed their example in turn, thus closing the door on any conceivable solution to the crisis. Both sides sought support among the rulers and population of Christendom, with the result that the split was extended far beyond the papal hierarchy, dividing all Europe into nearly equal camps. The English refused to pay allegiance to a French pope and were followed by the Flemish and a majority of the Germans and Italians. The French, however, were supported by the Spaniards, the Sicilians, and the Scots. Thus the balance was evenly weighted and neither side was forced or inclined to consider compromise.

With the ultimate source of Church authority hopelessly divided, clerical discipline was eroded by conflicting rulings and counter appeals. To many it seemed as if Christ's raiment had been permanently rent. In response the growing popular revulsion and despair, a council of cardinals, ostensibly drawn from all factions, was convened at Pisa. This body, in a bold attempt to break the impasse, deposed both popes in 1409 and attempted to replace them with a compromise candidate, who, being Greek, had not been implicated in the contest and was therefore possibly acceptable to all. Neither of the schismatic popes had the slightest intention of accepting the action of the

Council; and the new one died within a year. Undaunted by either the continued defiance of the
impenitent rivals or the demise of their new candidate, the cardinals of the Council insisted on their
canonical authority and made one more desperate
attempt to resolve the crisis. This time, instead of
seeking a neutral candidate, they selected the bellicose
and notorious cardinal-legate of Bologna, who took
office under the name of John XXIII.

Even though he was fully capable of protecting
the interests of the Pisan cardinals on the field of battle,
his record and reputation were hardly compatible
with his new position. By 1415, the public reaction
was such that he was finally brought to trial. "The
most scandalous charges were suppressed," the historian Gibbon later noted, ". . . the vicar of Christ
was only accused of piracy, murder, rape, sodomy
and incest." But what amused the sardonic Gibbon
did not amuse the devout and horrified world of the
later Middle Ages. Not only was he condemned and
deposed, but the revelations of the trial were so shocking that in spite of the fact that his name was ex-
punged from the list of popes, no subsequent pope
took the name of John again until our own day.

The Balance Sheet

To end a survey of the political developments of
the fourteenth century with an account of the apparent dissolution of the Church can only emphasize

the violent and chaotic character of the age. All the
great unifying concepts and institutions of Christendom seemed to be dissolving. Not only was the papacy fragmented, but Italy was a congeries of war-
ring states and cities, the Empire was disintegrating
into endless petty units, and even the French monarchy, weakened by war, a contested inheritance, and
the misrule of a mad king, appeared to be breaking
up. Only in England was the government sufficiently
strong and stable to maintain the territorial integrity
of the realm, but not, it should be added, to prevent
the growth of bitter factional rivalries which occasionally flared into open strife.

Given this general picture of incoherent parochial-
ism in so many aspects of European life, it is surprising to discover that some scholars have found significant beginnings of nationalism in the fourteenth century. This hypothesis, like the similar one that sees
origins of capitalism in the same period, must be considered with serious reservations. It is usually in con-
nection with the Hundred Years' War that the claim
for incipient national consciousness is made. The rav-
ages of incessant warfare drove the French to increasingly determined efforts at self-defense, at first local,
but eventually general. Inevitably these concerted attempts to pacify the country called attention to the
foreign character of the intruders and developed a
widespread hate of the English and perhaps some
premonitory signs of that love of France which a

little later was to find such remarkable embodiment in Joan of Arc. And it is possible that the English, by an obverse reaction, came to think of themselves as sharing a common "national" purpose in a foreign land. Even so, it is important to remember that in the early phases of the Hundred Years' War most of the English commanders still spoke French, and some at least saw themselves as future and rightful lords of French fiefs. Elsewhere in Europe loyalties were still predominantly local. Inhabitants of Florence, for example, considered themselves to be Florentine first, Tuscan second, and Italian last if at all. They would never have thought of burying their local animosities for the sake of the national good; and their contempt for their Pisan neighbors found eloquent expression in their habit of referring to both deceit and treason as "the Pisan vice." With the exception of England and France, there were few segments of Europe that could be considered "nations" in anything like the modern sense; and even in the exceptions, incipient nationalism can be detected only in primitive and intermittent manifestations.

Yet if many aspects of European life in the fourteenth century present a picture of incoherence, the all but overwhelming challenge presented by the forces of disintegration were often met with heroic courage. The great military victories of the period were won against tremendous odds; the most admired heroes were, like William Tell and Robert Bruce, courageous underdogs. Indeed, the story of Bruce and the spider, apocryphal though it may be, is an excellent symbolic summary of fourteenth-century history. Despite upheaval and turmoil, men did not give up hope for a better world. Reform and renovation were the basic preoccupations of the age. When it became clear, for example, that the Church had abdicated its leadership and that the future depended on the secular state, men responded by developing the patterns and foundations of stable modern government. Where viable constitutional patterns had been established, they were defended and maintained, and where new institutions were needed, they were improvised and elaborated. New bureaucracies, capable of carrying on the work of government in spite of disorder and disaster, burgeoned throughout Europe.

In spite of superficial indications to the contrary, the fourteenth century did not usher in a period as dark as that which followed either the collapse of Rome or of the Carolingian empire. Neither the deterioration of the once prosperous mediaeval economy nor the failure of the traditional political leadership destroyed the basic structure of European society. Severely tried, but far from defeated, the men of the period managed to preserve the most essential elements of their civilization and to reshape or replace what could not be maintained intact. That they did this in face of all but insurmountable adversity attests to both their resourcefulness and their determination.

CHAPTER III

Triumph ~~~~~~~~~~~~~~~~~~~

THE epitaph of a certain thirteenth-century theologian sums up a dominant intellectual attitude of the age. It said of him simply that "he knew all that there is to be known." The men of the thirteenth century felt so sure of themselves and their capacity to understand and make general statements about the nature of the world around them that there was no danger of this being taken as a jest. Such magnificent self-confidence, moreover, seemed to be fully justified by imposing achievement. Gothic cathedrals soared to the skies and dominated horizons in sharp contrast to earlier, earthbound structures. The sculpture and the glass of these awe-inspiring buildings told the whole story of men from the Creation to the Last Judgment and provided, as has often been said, an encyclopedia in pictures for those who could not read. For those who could read, encyclopedias in words were both plentiful and imposing, encompassing such subjects as history, natural history, law, and morals. Perhaps most impressive of all was the *Summa theologica* of

St. Thomas Aquinas, a great summary of theology
which endeavored to ask and answer, by the exercise
of human reason, a huge number of bewildering meta-
physical questions.

But in cultural matters, just as in economic and
political life, the thirteenth century may have pushed
too far too fast. While settlers, hungry for profits,
tried to cultivate marginal lands, and kings, thirsting
for power, demanded increasing obedience from their
subjects, cathedrals toward the end of the century
were built so high that they were either left unfinished or, as at Beauvais, actually collapsed. St. Thomas
died at the height of his powers, and one account reports that shortly before his death he abandoned
work on the *Summa*, saying "I cannot do it." The
harmonious and majestic reconciliation that had given
meaning and form to mediaeval civilization began to
crumble just as men found themselves struggling for
survival in the physical disarray of their society
brought on by famine, plague, and war. Disillusioned
by the moral and spiritual disintegration of the age,
they sought security and salvation with desperate energy and ingenuity.

Modern readers tend to view the self-confidence of
the thirteenth century with admiration and nostalgia,
even to the extent, on the part of a few, of deeming
the thirteenth the greatest of centuries in our entire
tradition. This is probably because the idea of know-
ing all that can be known is totally foreign to our

own intellectual powers or pretensions. In this attitude of mind we resemble the fourteenth century.
During that period of economic and political instability, men seldom found the traditional answers adequate to meet the crushing new problems that seemed
to arise on all sides. The change in mental attitude is
graphically illustrated by the fact that the *summa* or
summary, which had been a favorite compositional
form of the thirteenth century, was replaced in the
fourteenth century by the tract. This characteristic
form of writing was addressed to particular, often
practical, questions and written from all conceivable
points of view, conservative and progressive. In certain respects the age indeed gives the impression of
being intensely conservative and progressive at the
same time. Yet even reactionary approaches frequently arrived at conclusions that were new, and
with hindsight the fourteenth century can be seen as
a period of gestation for some distinctly modern ideas.
Such a view will be taken in this final chapter, but
with a warning to the reader to bear constantly in
mind that most "modern" movements were still minority movements and that the diversity of the age
defies most attempts at formulation.

Having said this, one must reiterate that the men
of the fourteenth century remained wholly mediaeval
—which is to say profoundly religious. This does not
mean that they were moral or pious, but that good or
bad, weak or strong, they accepted unquestioningly

the ultimate superiority of spiritual values in life. For this reason the humiliation of the papacy and the abuses of the clergy were traumatic. Their need for faith in God was if anything increased, with the result that the fourteenth century was a period of religious innovation in which many sought solace and salvation outside the established church. Those who did had the effective choice of attempting either to substitute intuitive religious experience (mysticism) for organized religious service or to develop their own personal formulation of necessary belief (heresy) in place of established dogma.

Mysticism

Mysticism had a long history within the development of Christianity. St. Augustine's *Confessions*, for example, radiate a mystical outlook, and the twelfth century produced one of the greatest mystics of all time in the person of St. Bernard. In the thirteenth century, however, mysticism was less prevalent because the mystic's search for God is intuitive and the age was fundamentally rational, preferring reason to intuition. The opposite was true of the fourteenth century, when rationalism was often questioned and mysticism became a dominant strain of European religiosity.

The first and greatest of the fourteenth-century mystics was the German Meister Eckhart (ca. 1260–1327), who, like St. Thomas Aquinas, was a member of the Dominican order. Eckhart was trained in the scholasticism of St. Thomas but went beyond scholasticism to the study of Neoplatonism. As another writer in this series has explained, "the Neoplatonists sought to be in touch with the absolute, with the eternal, which they conceived as lying behind all phenomena." [1] This striving for the union of the individual soul with the absolute became the major preoccupation of Meister Eckhart. Eckhart taught that by Divine Grace the essence of the soul, or "spark" as he called it, could be unified with God so long as the individual was prepared to dedicate himself entirely to this goal. Such an emphasis on the possibility of union between God and his creatures, however, verged dangerously near to pantheism and as a result Eckhart was condemned for heresy by the papal court at Avignon. This judgment has become the source of some controversy. Few scholars would deny that Eckhart's language was so paradoxical and ambiguous that it might have disquieted orthodox theologians. Yet it also seems clear that despite his startling language Eckhart had no heretical intentions.

Eckhart's German disciples, Johann Tauler (ca. 1300–1361) and Heinrich Suso (ca. 1295–1366), were more cautious. Suso, speaking constantly about the sorrows of Christ, placed himself in the center of the orthodox tradition. Both Suso and Tauler avoided

[1] Solomon Katz, *The Decline of Rome and the Rise of Mediaeval Europe* (Ithaca, N.Y., 1955), p. 41.

Eckhart's ambiguous references to the Trinity; they also divorced themselves from suspicions of pantheism by attacking pantheist heretics with great vigor, if not vituperation. A similar course was taken by mystics in other parts of Europe. In Flanders the great mystic Jan Ruysbroeck (1293–1381) followed the general pattern of Eckhart's thought but made a sharp and open break with pantheism, while in the South, mystics like the famous St. Catherine of Siena (1347–1380), acting without any direct relationship to the mysticism of the North, also pursued a more strictly orthodox and militant course.

The influence of this mystical current was manifold. Unlike earlier mystics, those of the fourteenth century were not content with pursuing their vision in seclusion and isolation. Eckhart and his followers had a message that they burned to share, and their most constant activity was the preaching of this message to as many people as would listen to it. Thus the most characteristic expressions of the movement were sermons composed and delivered in the German vernacular. These sermons take a pre-eminent place in the history of German culture because the constant use of German to express a complicated and ecstatic vision enriched the vernacular and helped to shape the course of German prose.

The spread of mysticism also resulted in an important movement for moral reform. Because the mystics insisted that union with God could be achieved only by the pure in heart, people became concerned with problems of morals and ethics. In Germany this concern helped to give purpose to life during a period of social incoherence. In addition, the practical aspect of the movement affected the course of education. Through the influence of Ruysbroeck, a community was established in Holland which educated the young in the so-called *Devotia moderna*, or new devotion. This Dutch community was to train some of the leading thinkers of future generations including the great Christian Humanist Erasmus. Mysticism also had an indisputable link with the Protestant Reformation. While men like Suso and Tauler were careful to insist upon their orthodoxy, their message stressed an inner response which by implication could easily be extended to a contempt for outward forms such as the sacraments. Tauler himself referred to the "inward-looking man" and declared that "churches make no man holy, but men make churches holy." The perpetuation of such sentiments helped to foster a gradual alienation from the Church and cultivated the harvest that was later to be reaped by Martin Luther.

Heresy

Most of the fourteenth-century mystics remained in the orthodox camp and were generally careful to avoid conflict with Church dogma. But criticism, of course, went further and frequently resulted in heresy. Indeed, throughout the century heresy posed a great problem and challenge for Church discipline and Christian life.

The most radical challenge was offered by the heresy of the Free Spirit. This movement had existed in the thirteenth century, but became truly dangerous only after the papacy had moved to Avignon. There is not much accurate information regarding the beliefs of the devotees of the Free Spirit because most of their writings were efficiently consigned to the flames. Yet the major outlines of the heretical program are clear. The fundamental tenet was that man could achieve deification by his own decision and without the aid of Divine Grace. Free Spirit heretics claimed godlike powers and declared that they had reached a state of sinlessness which rendered traditional morality irrelevant. This doctrine was probably the most radical attack on tradition that the Middle Ages had ever known. Standard moral precepts were turned upside down as Free Spirit heretics proclaimed unrestrained sexual license and tried to justify idleness and theft. Whether the Free Spirit heretics actually practiced what they preached is a question that is nearly impossible to answer, but merely preaching such a doctrine was a sufficient threat to orthodoxy. Furthermore, its followers were surprisingly well organized and were able to spread their ideas from France to Austria and from Holland to Italy. Naturally the Church did its best to uproot this growth and by the fifteenth century had largely succeeded. But the initial success of the movement was a significant symptom of the times and an important harbinger of the future.

Entirely different from the heresy of the Free Spirit was the English heresy of John Wyclif (ca. 1330–1384). In his early career as a professor at the University of Oxford, Wyclif was known only as a scholar who enjoyed complicated theological arguments. If he had lived in another, happier age he might have spent his life in dry, scholarly disputes. But in the late fourteenth century England was becoming a hotbed of anticlericalism. For one thing, the client popes of the French monarchy were making constant and exigent demands for money. By no means eager to meet these papal exactions, the English aristocracy challenged the authority of the Avignonese papacy and sought support in latent anticlericalism and such a potent spokesman as Wyclif.

Wyclif based his attacks on the clergy on a position diametrically opposed to that of the Free Spirit heresy. While the latter argued that man could become divine by his own decision and without intervention of Grace, Wyclif stressed the saving power of Grace and the fundamental sinfulness of man. According to Wyclif, no man could claim absolute power or dominion without the gift of Grace. This limitation he extended even to the priestly office and priests, including popes; those who were not in a state of Grace were according to Wyclif no priests at all. With the popes in Avignon and the clergy becoming more and more embroiled in secular affairs, this doctrine attracted much favorable attention and support. But as Wyclif grew older he became more radical. In his later writings he attacked the very existence of Church government, not just its unworthy servants, and argued that true Christian life depended on a return to the literal rather than the customary allegorical interpretation of the Bible, which meant, in this context, the elimination of the clerical hierarchy. Finally, just before he died, he attacked the doctrine of the Eucharist, which conferred on priests, worthy or not, the exclusive right to administer this central sacrament of the Church, a monopoly for which he found no authority in the records of the apostolic tradition. From a plea for radical reform Wyclif had moved to a direct challenge of the most fundamental dogma of the church. His influential supporters, hardly prepared for open heresy, began to be disaffected. If he had lived longer he might have faced severe penalties, but he died unharmed before the tide had fully turned against him.

The heresy of Wyclif was notable for a number of reasons. Before the late fourteenth century, England had been a stronghold of orthodoxy and was remarkably immune from heretical infection. Thus Wyclif's successful career in the most orthodox of countries was an impressive testimony to the weakening of

Church discipline and the burgeoning criticism of traditional standards and dogmas. More specifically Wyclif's insistence on a literal interpretation of the Bible led to a translation of the Bible into English. The vernacular Wyclifite Bible was copied frequently and had an important influence on the development of the English language as well as on the development of English piety.

If Wyclif's growing intransigence toward the end of his life cost him his aristocratic support, it earned him a sizable following among the lower classes. After his death, these followers, known as "Lollards," were persecuted and went underground until they were able to take up their criticism openly once more during the time of the Protestant Reformation. Wyclif's views were also carried by Czech scholars to Bohemia, where they had more obvious success. Transplanted in Bohemia, Wyclif's example stimulated and encouraged John Hus (1370–1416) in developing the heresy which exerted a great influence on central Europe throughout the fifteenth century and which was another important forerunner of the Protestant Reformation.

Nominalism and Political Thought

Beside the introspective reformism of the mystics, the radical reformism of the Free Spirit heretics, and the near Protestant reformism of the Wyclifites, the remarkable diversity of fourteenth-century thought

and criticism was rounded out by the logical reformism
of the nominalist movement. The major tenets of nominalism were no more new to the fourteenth century
than were the other previously mentioned movements. What was new was the rigor with which they
were driven to their ultimate conclusions and the
train of highly significant consequences which this
procedure produced.

The great fourteenth-century exponent of nominalism was an English Franciscan by the name of
William of Ockham (ca. 1295–1349). In the later
Middle Ages, the Franciscans competed openly and
often passionately with their rival order, the Domini-
cans. In the realm of philosophy, this meant that
Franciscan scholars tended to exploit the inherent
contradictions in the magnificent theoretical edifice
of the Dominican school. Brought to its greatest perfection by St. Thomas Aquinas in his *Summa theologica,* it was organized on the principle that human
reason is generally compatible with faith. For example, St. Thomas tried to demonstrate that such a
basic proposition of Christian faith as the existence of
God could be proved by human reason. Ockham, on
the other hand, contended that a sharp division had
to be made between reason and faith. According to
him, human beings could only be certain about
knowledge obtained by direct experience received
through intuition or the senses and that such experience could only perceive particulars and not general

categories. For Ockham, therefore, the great scholastic categories were mere names (in Latin, *nomina*, whence the term nominalism) and could not—as his opponents maintained—be made the subject of human science. The most important of these general categories was, of course, the idea of God; and Ockham, following his argument to its logical conclusion, insisted that knowledge of God could properly be sought not through human science but only in revealed theology. Human science, that is, should no more concern itself with theology or metaphysics than theology should interfere with such human sciences as grammar, logic, or physics. By this simple but devastating formula, the elaborate synthesis constructed by St. Thomas was torn down and reduced to fragments.

Self-evident as Ockham's view will seem to us— since it is axiomatic to modern science—nominalism never became more than a minority movement in the fourteenth century. Its ramifications, however, were frequently far more widespread and important than the number of its followers would suggest, and its implications often seemed to be reflected in some of the characteristic tendencies of the age. Nominalism, for example, with its stress on earthly knowledge susceptible of dispassionate proof, might seem to provide little place for mysticism; but its very insistence that knowledge of God was irrational and could not be approached by human science left this ultimate problem to the subjective methods cultivated by the mystics. In this context it is interesting to point out that Martin Luther, who—though no mystic—was to affirm the subjectivity of religion and to denounce the teachings of St. Thomas, was to be educated in the nominalist University of Erfurt and to refer to William of Ockham as his "dear master."

Nominalism also had a great influence on the development of political theory. Ockham himself was not content to pass his life within the confines of a university. He became actively engaged in politics and took the side of the Franciscans in their attacks on papal worldliness. As a result he was condemned and forced to flee to the court of the Pope's leading enemy, Emperor Louis of Bavaria, where he joined other refugees from papal wrath who served as propagandists for the imperial cause. One of the most original and effective of these was Marsiglio of Padua (ca. 1275–1343), whose ideas were similar to Ockham's but whose writing was less obscured by difficult language and whose conclusions were far more revolutionary.

Marsiglio of Padua's major work was the *Defensor pacis* (*Defender of the Peace*), written in collaboration with the Parisian scholar John of Jandun in 1324. Probably the most significant contribution to political theory written in the later Middle Ages, it attacked the theory of a united Christian community ruled over by the pope. As Ockham had argued for a separation between the spheres of faith and human science, so Marsiglio argued for a separation between spiritual and secular authority. Marsiglio, however, did not rest with the theory of two coordinate powers, but went on to insist that the Church should be subordinated to the state. The clergy, according to Marsiglio, were simply members of the state whose special function was to teach and interpret scripture. In all other matters he considered them to be no different from other classes in society and claimed that they should therefore be subject to secular authority.

In addition to defending the superiority of the secular to the spiritual, Marsiglio also developed some striking constitutional ideas about the nature of the state itself. The ultimate source of authority, he declared, rested among the better citizens of the state, who should shape the laws. It was the function of the monarch merely to enforce them; and if he failed in this responsibility or exceeded his authority, he was simply to be replaced. In modern terms this meant that Marsiglio wanted the executive to be placed in a position subordinate to the legislature.

This formulation, a moderate constitutional theory, with its explicit statement of separation of powers, sounds very modern; and indeed it was too advanced for the fourteenth century. That it earned its authors excommunication was hardly surprising, considering its implications for the papacy, but it is perhaps strange that it did not attract more secular attention

—it was not widely read—since much of it only described existing conditions. Rulers like Edward I and Philip the Fair had already succeeded in subordinating the Church to the state on occasion, and bodies of prominent citizens had begun to exercise constitutional checks on the monarch in England and many other parts of Europe. But theory in the Middle Ages often lagged behind practice; and a candid statement of a new position, such as the *Defensor pacis*, was frequently taken to be more shocking than was its practical implementation. In retrospect, it is clear that the *Defensor* was truly epoch-making. Not only were all opponents of papal supremacy from Wyclif to the reformers of the sixteenth century to turn to it for theoretical ammunition, but it announced an emphasis on secular politics that was to become a characteristic trait of the modern world.

Nominalism and Natural Science

One of the most remarkable achievements of the fourteenth century was the development of new scientific theories by groups of scholars at the universities of Oxford and Paris. Gradually they began to question the assumptions of the Aristotelian and mediaeval world view and to formulate theories, which if not fully modern, constituted important departures from existing traditions. Before we examine the details of this achievement, and the possible influence it may have had on scientists of the sixteenth and seven-

teenth centuries, it will be worthwhile to note that
it, too, was related to a nominalistic attitude. Not all
the fourteenth-century scientists were Ockhamists,
but unquestionably the nominalist view of knowledge
created a more favorable atmosphere for scientific
thought.

Throughout the Middle Ages most men regarded
the natural world as a mirror of Divine Truths. They
believed that the universe could be read as a book
revealing Divine purpose; and they studied natural
objects, not for their unique qualities, but as symbols
of something greater. Men thought, for example, that
lion cubs were born dead and came to life on the
third day as symbols of Christ's Resurrection. Such
an approach may have served poetry, but it hampered
scientific speculation because it supplied theological
generalization in place of critical observation. Nominalism, on the other hand, dissolved such symbolic
"truths" into tangible particulars. The nominalists
were determined to find a limited body of knowledge
that could be regarded as certain; and they rejected
all abstractions which did not conform with direct
intuition. This approach led them to open up entirely
new scientific vistas.

Important contributions to science, however, were
made long before Ockham. In the thirteenth century,
the great age of Dominican theology at Paris, a group
of scholars associated with the Franciscan order at
Oxford turned their attention to mathematics and

science. The first, Robert Grosseteste, did impressive work in geometry and optics, and inspired many students. The foremost of these was Roger Bacon— an erratic genius whose work sometimes foreshadowed experimental method but who was largely misunderstood in his own day. This tradition of scientific study at Oxford was carried on in the fourteenth century by a group of scholars at Merton College, notably Thomas Bradwardine. These men not only made important contributions to the study of mathematics but developed an interest in problems of motion that was soon picked up by others at Paris.

It can be seen, then, that scientific interest was by no means exclusively dependent on the philosophy of Ockham, but it was at Paris, in a distinctively Ockhamist atmosphere, that the most impressive fourteenth-century work was done. The Parisian theorists started with the physics of Aristotle and regarded themselves as Aristotelians, but in commenting on the master they made important modifications which proved to be the first step in the break-away from classical views which culminated in the work of Galileo and Newton. Most important was their new work on motion. All previous theorizing about this subject had derived from the physics of Aristotle, which began with a fundamental distinction between vertical, or "natural," and horizontal, or "forced," motion. This latter was explained as the result of constant pushing. A projectile, that is, was believed to be propelled by an original violent movement which was sustained by continuing disturbances in the air. Such an explanation could not withstand the simplest common-sense analysis. If two archers shot at each other, their arrows passing in flight would have to be propelled, according to the Aristotelians, by the movement of air in opposite directions. This was so palpably absurd that some mediaeval philosophers had introduced invisible spirits to help push the objects along when the Aristotelian rush of air failed.

To the Parisian nominalists this was an unacceptable solution and, to replace it, they developed a theory of "impetus." Its principal exponent, John Buridan (ca. 1300–ca. 1358), held that an object was kept in motion by means of an "impetus" which was imprinted on it by the original moving force. This theory, it was soon realized, had startling implications for the then accepted explanations of the rotation of heavenly bodies. Aristotelian cosmologists, who could account for motion only by the continuous action of a mover, had argued that the heavenly bodies were imbedded in transparent spheres which were moved around the earth by means of "intelligences" or, in Christian terms, angels. With their concept of impetus, however, the Parisians could eliminate the need for such occult forces. God, they asserted, impressed an initial impetus on the heavenly bodies which set them turning in an uninterrupted and perpetual orbit. If this explanation did not fully encompass the modern law of inertia, it did anticipate it to some extent. More important, it eliminated the need for special, or divine, intervention to explain the working of the universe and thus prepared the way for the more sophisticated researches of Leonardo da Vinci and Galileo.

Another original and resourceful thinker in the Parisian group was Nicolas of Oresme (ca. 1330– 1382), a pupil of Buridan as well as a bishop and a friend and adviser of the French king Charles V. Nicolas went so far as to describe the universe as a mechanical clock, originally created and set in motion by God and then left to run by itself, thus foreshadowing the mechanistic thought of the eighteenth-century, post-Newtonian world. Nicolas' book on cosmology, written like so many other important works of the century in the vernacular, further suggested the then radical theory that the earth rotates diurnally on its axis. Nor were Nicolas' interests confined to cosmology; he was, in fact, one of the most versatile geniuses of the later Middle Ages. For example, in his efforts to clarify and communicate some highly abstract and characteristically mediaeval concepts concerning "forms" and "qualities," he developed diagramatic visual aids that suggested later graphic techniques of representing mathematical relationships; these suggest to some modern scholars that he may have anticipated analytical geometry. He also wrote a tract on coinage which became one of the earliest scientific studies of monetary and fiscal problems.

If the fourteenth-century school of Paris was so advanced, why, then, did its members not go ahead to draw what were later to seem the obvious practical conclusions from their theories? This is a perplexing problem, but the basic answer seems to be that the Parisian scholars were still very mediaeval in the sense that they were far more concerned with speculative philosophy than with demonstrable theories. They were not interested in performing experiments, let alone investigating the practical applications that might have derived from their speculations. It was this frame of mind which separated them furthest from the practical orientation of modern science. But their influence was still profound, and their theories continued to be taught until the sixteenth century. Moreover, by 1400, Europeans were the only men in the world who were working on science with constant interest and application, thus replacing such earlier leaders in scientific research as the Chinese, Hindus, and Moslems.

Technology

If the nominalist scholars of the fourteenth century were not interested in the possible practical applications of their theories, there were other men, usually anonymous, who were actively concerned with technology and who had a much greater immediate impact on daily life in Europe. War has frequently stimulated technological development and the endless conflicts of the fourteenth century were no exception. We have already seen how the English longbow gave its masters a decisive superiority in the Hundred Years' War. Far more significant for the future, though less effective at the time, were the advances made in firearms. By 1300, Europeans had developed reasonably advanced methods of casting metals and had acquired formulae for gunpowder. The result was the cannon. The earliest European picture of this novel weapon dates from 1327 and shows it shooting an arrow rather than a ball. But Europeans learned fast. The English probably used cannon at the battle of Crécy in 1346 and certainly used it for sieges as early as 1339. Soon it was considered standard military equipment, and smaller guns were developed during the same period. Needless to say, it was often more dangerous to stand behind than in front of some of these primitive weapons. Even so, once the initial discoveries had been made, improvements were only a matter of time; and with the introduction of firearms, the nature of warfare was to be revolutionized.

If the technology of destruction was of paramount importance to the men of the fourteenth century, they still did not neglect the possibilities of improving the instruments and techniques used in peaceful pursuits. One important area of innovation was in the construction and handling of ships. It was in this period that Europeans began to build ships sturdy enough to take to the open ocean and manageable enough to work slightly into the wind. The ability to hold a general course at sea, made possible by the invention of the mariner's compass and the consequent development of accurate nautical charts and maps, produced a revolution in sailing. Navigators no longer needed to rely on clear skies in order to guide their voyages by means of the sun and the stars. With reliable charts and navigational instruments ships could sail in the winter long after the skies had become overcast. Nor were they forced to hug the shores for fear of getting lost. By the fourteenth century, Italian ships were beginning to break out of the Mediterranean. The famous Venetian galleys were passing the Straits of Gibraltar and making their way up the coast to England and Flanders. Others seem to have ventured out on the high seas to reach the Canary and Madeira islands. These bold forays into the Atlantic not only presaged the voyages of Columbus; they established the techniques which made them possible. Indeed, Columbus himself relied so heavily on sailing by compass that he really had no accurate idea of how to sail by the sun and stars.

The perfection of map and chart making was only one aspect of a widespread interest in the technology of measurement. In addition to developing methods for measuring space and distance, men of the fourteenth century also succeeded in making instruments to measure time. In the early Middle Ages, men had relied on sundials for this purpose, and when the sun failed to shine they fell back on a variety of running-down devices. Alfred the Great, for example, in the ninth century, bothered by the problem of keeping time at night, had resorted to burning down knotched candles. It was not until late in the thirteenth century, however, that Europeans became sufficiently familiar with mechanical techniques to improve substantially upon this simple solution by devising a mechanical clock using geared wheels and escape mechanisms. In the fourteenth century, when craftsmen had mastered the art sufficiently to produce reliable mechanical clocks in some quantity, these became something of a fad. Elaborate clocks in public buildings became status symbols, and communities vied with each other in installing mechanisms which would not only tell time but also perform complicated tricks as they struck the hours, thus inaugurating a tradition that finds its modern expression in the baseball scoreboard that explodes with euphoria every time the home team scores a home run. With the perfection of clocks, Europeans began to divide the hour into sixty minutes and the minute into sixty seconds. Thus one of the most characteristic aspects of Western civilization—the preoccupation with exact time measurement—was born.

Other technological advances of the fourteenth century can only be mentioned in passing. Around the year 1300, eyeglasses made their first appearance in western Europe. Students of optics also became more familiar with laws of perspective, which, as we will see, had a great influence on the history of art.

Practical medicine also progressed in the fourteenth century. Very slowly after the Black Death, techniques of sanitation, quarantine, and post-mortem dissection became more prevalent. Many men still regarded the dissection of a human body as tantamount to dissecting God, but Italian and French physicians pursued their investigations despite this prejudice and the opprobrium it engendered. Even so, the anatomical charts that resulted from their research were far inferior to the nautical charts used by mariners. But the need for exact observation and measurement in medicine was becoming evident.

Fine Arts

Not surprisingly, the age that recognized a need for exact observation and measurement was also the one that produced a revolution in art. This revolution clearly corresponded to the spectacular advances in technology, theoretical science, and philosophic outlook that occurred during the fourteenth century. The technology of measurement and the growing interest in anatomy helped to stimulate an artistic interest in human proportions; the study of optics and new departures in geometry led to the first awareness of the problem of perspective; and the nominalist view of examining particular conditions, rather than general types, helped to prepare the way for artistic naturalism. Such powerful influences could hardly have failed to affect the development of painting; but acting through the genius of the great Italian painter Giotto, they produced a major artistic revolution.

Giotto (ca. 1266–1336) is commonly regarded as one of the most remarkable figures in the history of culture. A shepherd who left his flocks to become the first truly great painter of the postclassical world, he liberated Italian art from the dominating influence of Byzantine formalism and left it pre-eminent in Europe. Giotto's contemporaries credited him with having been the first to imitate nature in a realistic manner. Previously, mediaeval artists were preoccupied with abstractions, and their art, two-dimensional and highly symbolic, was intended to capture the "ideas" or "essences" of objects rather than their actual appearance. Giotto, in contrast, tried to represent space in depth and became one of the first to take account of the problem of perspective in painting. His work also portrayed everyday subjects, running the gamut from family scenes to dramatic situations, all fraught with human emotions. His representations of St. Francis, for example, reveal the humanity of his subject in a way that was entirely new to the Middle Ages. This is not at all to say that Giotto strove for photographic realism. Many of his finest works depicted allegorical figures and supernatural events, but in the same natural manner he used for mundane sub-jects. So great was this gift that Boccaccio insisted Giotto's painting could deceive the senses.

Giotto's style was immediately copied in his native city of Florence and influenced important painters in the neighboring city of Siena, who, in elegance of line, rapidly surpassed even Giotto himself. By the middle of the century there was a temporary reaction in the form of a revival of symbolic and mystical themes, accompanied by a preoccupation with death and damnation most likely brought about by the Black Death and the other upheavals of the age. For a while this renewed preoccupation with abstractions replaced the simple naturalness of Giotto. Not long afterwards, Italian artists returned to his principles, which, in the fifteenth century, they were to perfect in one of the most spectacular periods of artistic cre-ativity ever known to man.

Nor was Giotto's influence limited to Italy. The Italian experiment with perspective spread rapidly to the North, where it was employed in the art of manu-script illumination. Interestingly, the new techniques were first adopted in Paris—the home of nominalism and theoretical science. About 1325, Jean Pucelle, a Frenchman who is sometimes called "the Giotto of the North," began to use perspective and psychologi-cal expression in his manuscript illuminations. Pucelle also delighted in filling his pages with a profusion of natural objects. His own signature was the punning device of a dragonfly, which in mediaeval French was called *pucelle*. Other French illuminators, following Pucelle's initiative, began to illustrate the seasons through rudimentary but three-dimensional landscapes instead of conventional allegorical figures. By the end of the century, the painters of the North had so fully assimilated perspective and the other new techniques as to rival their Italian teachers. They soon began to teach them in turn, ultimately producing, through this exchange of influences, the so-called International Style.

Another highly significant innovation of fourteenth-century art was the development of the portrait. There were no portrait painters in the high Middle Ages because men were less interested in individual personality traits than they were in idealized representations of significant moral types. Sitting for a portrait would have been regarded as a cardinal example of the sin of pride. During the fourteenth century, however, the cult of fame became a dominant literary theme, just as the claims of the particular were slowly replacing the claims of the universal, providing an impetus as well as a favorable climate for the revival of the long-neglected portrait genre. Representations of distinctive facial features for the purpose of revealing character can first be discerned in sculpture. A life-size portrait bust of Pope Boniface VIII executed early in the century is recognized as the first representation of a pope that can be regarded as an accurate personal likeness. The greater plasticity of the three-dimensional form undoubtedly lent itself more readily to portraiture, but painting was pressed into the same service later in the century. The earliest known example, dating from about 1360, is a striking portrait of the French king John the Good painted on canvas stretched over wood. Soon it became customary for important men to have painters fix their likenesses as a means of obtaining worldly immortality. As a result, it is in the fourteenth century that students of mediaeval history can identify notables as truly animated beings rather than mysterious figures shrouded by blurred effigies.

Vernacular Literature

Still another example of the breakdown of universal forms in the fourteenth century was the accelerated decline of the use of Latin in favor of the European vernaculars. Even though vernacular literature had made its appearance in Europe as early as the twelfth century, a strong predisposition toward Latin for professional or academic writing lingered on. Thus, in the thirteenth century, romances, histories, and lyric poems, in short those genres intended primarily to entertain, were increasingly written in the vernacular; but philosophy, theology, law, and politics, serious subjects treated by scholars and directed to an international professional audience, were still usually presented in Latin. In the fourteenth century, however, officials started to keep administrative records in the vernacular, and philosophers and scientists like Oresme used it for some of their most influential treatises. As the great religious controversies of the age became matters of general public concern, they too were conducted increasingly in the vernacular. The German mystics, as we have already seen, preached and wrote in it; and radical reformers like Wyclif advocated its use in translations.

At the same time, the development of vernacular literature reached a new stage with the appearance of writings that can take their place with the greatest masterworks of the world. Foremost among these is the *Divine Comedy* of Dante (1265–1321). This long allegorical poem describing the pilgrimage and salvation of the Christian soul was written as its author, a political exile from his native Florence, wandered through northern Italy seeking patronage and asylum. Considering these circumstances, one might expect the *Divine Comedy* to be morose and bitter. Instead, it rises above Dante's immediate concerns to make one of the most elevated statements about man's relation to the universe. It is still the universe of St. Thomas's *Summa* (to which the *Comedy* has often been compared) but with the academic prose transmuted into soaring verse. But even if his work is mediaeval in its inspiration and orientation, as scholars of literature insist, Dante seems, like Giotto, to surpass the traditional limits of the mediaeval world, an impression that may be due in part to his stupendous genius. In his hands, for example, as in Giotto's, traditional allegorical abstractions became intensely human figures. In this and other ways Dante and Giotto were simply too great to be fitted completely into any category, even one so commodious as "mediaeval."

Further, even if Dante's basic assumptions were mediaeval, his judgments frequently revealed a concern with humanity different from that found in traditional theology. In contrast to the *Summa* of St. Thomas, Dante's poem appeals more to the emotions than to the intellect. Where St. Thomas attempted to reconcile faith and reason, Dante evoked hope and fear, and stressed conduct more than belief, as shown by the presence of a controversial mediaeval prophet and a heretic in his *Paradise*. Thus Dante repeatedly veers away from the logical dogmatism found in scholastic philosophy toward the humane and ethical interest in man that was to characterize and illuminate the literature of the Renaissance. Finally, of course, Dante's style is so original and powerful that it left a lasting imprint on Italian as a literary language.

In the development of Italian literature, Dante is followed by Petrarch (1304–1374) and Boccaccio (1313–1375), who with him comprise the so-called "three crowns of Tuscany." All were products of the mediaeval tradition, but each in turn looks further away from the cultural synthesis of the thir-

teenth century which had been their common heri-
tage. Petrarch like Dante was a wanderer. Born in
Tuscany but forced to spend even more of his life
than Dante in travels, he wrote in nearly every literary and philosophical genre during his long career.
His huge output is at once the delight and despair of
scholars because he had the engaging but exasperating
habit of frequently changing his point of view. But if
his beliefs are elusive, many of his traits of character
are clear. Even more than Dante, he subordinated
questions of theological dogma to considerations of
human morality. This preoccupation drove him to
denounce the—to him—arid philosophy of the mediaeval schools and to study and attempt to emulate
the great classical moralists such as Cicero. Petrarch's
profound knowledge of, and love for, Cicero and his
sentimental attachment to Plato (whom he could not
read because he knew no Greek) helped to initiate
the great Italian cult of antiquity which reached its
climax in the next century.

Petrarch did not, as is often thought, turn to the
classics as an alternative to Christianity. Instead he
believed that Ciceronian ethics were essentially Christian, and he loved the moral writings of St. Augustine
as much as those of Cicero. Nonetheless, Petrarch's
concern for moral philosophy led him to stress the
role of man in the world. He was, as a result, a con-
vert to the new cult of fame to the extent of having
himself crowned with laurel on the Capitoline Hill

at Rome in 1342—a gesture that his favorite, St. Augustine, could hardly have condoned. Petrarch wrote beautiful sonnets and songs in the vernacular and thus enriched the Italian language, but he thought less of these than of his own works in Latin and considered his vernacular compositions to have been trifling. His is a fascinating character and he emerges from his numerous writings and letters as a genuine personality. Indeed, he is one of the earliest literary figures to step out of the shadows and reveal his inner self. For this reason Petrarch, despite all his mediaeval residues, has been called the first modern man.

Boccaccio, the last of the three great Italian writers of the fourteenth century, was also a Tuscan. A close friend of Petrarch and an admirer of Dante, on whom he lectured in his native city, Boccaccio wrote in a manner quite foreign to the tastes of either of his predecessors. Eschewing their elevated tone, Boccaccio developed his own worldly style carefully attuned to the rhythms of colloquial speech and suited to the description of commonplace events. His greatest work, the *Decameron*, is, as the title suggests, a collection of ten units of ten stories each. The object is the elegant entertainment of his well-born and well-bred contemporaries. The language is therefore their own vernacular and the style is lucid and charming. The subjects are diverse—ranging from tragedy to farce—but each tale bears witness to the author's passion to please as well as to his great literary talent, so that in both purpose and style the *Decameron* is a fresh departure from tradition as well as a model for all future storytellers.

Italian writers, like Italian painters, were pre-eminent throughout the fourteenth century, but the emergence and growth of vernacular literatures was a phenomenon as wide as Europe. France, which had led in the development of the mediaeval Gothic style, was slow in accepting Italian literary models and, in fact, during the fourteenth century French literature languished. Nonetheless the vernacular gained in currency and force in unlikely places. Professors at the University of Orléans, for example, began to lecture in French instead of Latin, and one of the greatest works of French history—the *Chronicle* of Jean Froissart (ca. 1337–1404)—was written in a vernacular style unparalleled for its clarity and grace.

More striking developments occurred in England, where English began to replace French as the principal literary language for the first time since the Norman Conquest. In the early fourteenth century, the English nobility spoke French, and French replaced Latin as the language of law and government; but as the Hundred Years' War progressed English slowly replaced French as both the written and spoken language of the entire country. Even so, in the period of transition people frequently wrote a curious mixture of the two languages. The following extract of a letter dating from the early part of Richard II's reign offers a sample:

Treschere cosyn, ieo vous pry bryng a wryt of trespas en ver Richard forde of Sulyhul, Wyliam of Noryng of Yzerdeley, Wilyam Ducy of Northfield, the wheche trespas hu duden the waley of twenty mark touching to me and my tenante.[1]

(My dear cousin, I beg you to bring a writ of trespass against Richard Ford of Solihull, William Noring of Yardley, William Ducy of Northfield, the said trespass they did to the value of twenty marks against me and my tenant.)

Such curious and halting attempts were to be expected in an age of transition. At the same time, however, several poets were using English most effectively as a literary vehicle. The greatest among them, Geoffrey Chaucer (ca. 1340–1400), was probably the only writer of the century who could take his place beside Dante, Petrarch, and Boccaccio. Chaucer borrowed heavily from Petrarch and Boccaccio for some of his plots, and his most familiar work, the *Canterbury Tales,* is in some ways strikingly similar to the *Decameron.* Yet Chaucer apparently never read Boccaccio's masterpiece and can by no means be considered a mere imitator. His characters have a life of

[1] Letter from Rose Mountefort to her cousin, quoted by H. S. Bennett, *Chaucer and the Fifteenth Century* (Oxford, 1947), pp. 177–178.

their own, and the English setting of the *Canterbury Tales* is quite as authentic and original as the Italian setting of the *Decameron*. Chaucer's language, too, although taken from the common speech of London, was transformed by his verse in a way that did as much to shape the literary development of English as did that of the three great Tuscans to shape Italian. Nor is Chaucer a mere figure of literary history. College students faced with an assignment from the *Canterbury Tales* are often surprised to find that Chaucer is one of the most entertaining writers of all time.

History

A book devoted to the history of the fourteenth century might well end with a glance at the fourteenth-century view of history. The first thing to notice is that it was in no sense a period of innovation in form; its greatest histories are notable either for their vivid style, as in Froissart's *Chronicle*, or for their careful attention to detail, as in Villani's *History of Florence*. But they remain characteristically mediaeval, copying traditional models and displaying the most obvious of established prejudices. It is thus not to the historians but rather to men of letters, and particularly Petrarch, that one must look for a fresh view of history. Indeed it was just because his passionate interest in the classical past was focused on literature, rather than conventional history, that he arrived at such original and significant conclusions.

Mediaeval men, it has been said with justice, had a very strong sense of historical continuity but a very weak sense of historical perspective. They did not consider classical times to have been remote or different; indeed most of them believed that the Roman Empire had never really fallen but continued on into their own day. Such a view led to considerable confusion. One manuscript, for example, shows the god Mercury dressed as a fourteenth-century bishop. Mediaeval thinkers, that is, simply did not recognize the fact that they lived in what we now call the "Middle Ages." It was Petrarch who, in his love for the classical spirit, first insisted that with the fall of Rome an age of darkness had descended upon the world and had lasted until his own century. He thus implicitly divided history into the three familiar categories of ancient, mediaeval, and modern.

This new approach to history had a tremendous impact. Following Petrarch's lead, scholars began to study classical antiquity with fewer preconceptions and strictly as a discrete phenomenon of the past. Even more important, the division of history into three distinct ages made possible an optimistic view of man's destiny. Where their mediaeval predecessors had been convinced that the world was growing old and was about to end, the Italian writers of the fourteenth century spoke incessantly about rejuvenation and rebirth. They believed that Giotto had rediscovered the art of painting and Dante and Petrarch had rediscovered the art of writing. No doubt this view was limited to Italy and no doubt even there it was held only by a small elite. No doubt, too, most Europeans throughout the fourteenth century were pessimistic and preoccupied with death. Yet as time went on, the conviction that they were living on the threshold of a great revival began to spread among an increasing number of educated Italians. These men believed that they were the harbingers of a Golden Age. Considering the many achievements snatched from the all but overwhelming adversities of the fourteenth century, perhaps they were right.

Epilogue

THERE was no jubilee in the year 1400. By that time the papacy had been split for twenty-two years and the situation looked more hopeless than ever. The rival popes, supported by their respective cardinals, had no intention of compromising, and the only chance for undercutting them seemed to lie in an agreement among the secular powers. But many of the major European states were at war with each other and all of them lacked the charismatic leadership needed to deal firmly with the problem.

A curious anecdote illustrates the plight of Europe at that time. In 1398, while the rival claimants to the papal chair were hurling anathemas at each other, the King of France and the Emperor of Germany decided to meet in an attempt to heal the Schism. Yet unfortunately each had his own weakness. Charles VI of France was a well-meaning man, but he suffered from periodic bouts of madness, while the Emperor Wenceslas, known by one tradition as the "Good," was truly good at only one thing and that was drinking. Charles was not often lucid, but his brain was usually clearer in the afternoon after he had digested a good meal. By that time, however, Wenceslas had started drinking and there was no talking to him. Thus the two monarchs never succeeded in communicating and the meetings were adjourned, leaving the Church as divided and Christendom as demoralized as before.

If this bizarre tale is accepted as a symbol of the dismal end of the fourteenth century, the contrast between the opening and the end of the period becomes immediately evident. In 1300, Rome seemed the capital of the world and Europeans seemed self-confident; in 1400, Rome was the outpost of a discredited papal faction and Europeans seemed exhausted by years of plague and war. Yet appearances were deceiving. As we have seen, the splendid jubilee of Pope Boniface VIII was an end rather than a beginning, for the decades after 1300 saw first the collapse of the universal papacy and then the coming of a time of troubles for the secular states. After 1400, on the other hand, the European situation slowly began to improve. In 1417, the papal schism was finally healed by the Council of Constance and unity was restored to Christendom. At the same time the attacks of plague began to taper off and both economic and political stability slowly returned to Europe. Italy was the first area to recover and push ahead in an outburst of creative enthusiasm that shaped one of the most glorious ages in her history.

Northern Europe followed more slowly. There war hampered the growth of the economy and aggravated political instability until the last decades of the fifteenth century. Thereafter, however, in a very short space of time the North rapidly outstripped Italy in economic, political, and cultural development and began to spread its hegemony over the globe.

How does the fourteenth century fit into this pattern? Was the age merely an intermission between the acts of mediaeval and modern accomplishment? In a sense it was, but it was also more than that. In the fourteenth century the civilization of the high Middle Ages was tested. Much that lacked durability was cast aside, but with great determination the men of the age held on to many of the positive mediaeval accomplishments and saved Europe from total collapse. At the same time adversity led to the shaping of new forms and ideas where they were needed, and many of them were passed on to the succeeding ages. None of us would have liked to have lived in the fourteenth century, for it was a trying period, but we may be glad that the men of that age who were so tried were not found wanting.

Chronological Summary~~~~~~~~~

1272–1307	Edward I, king of England
1285–1314	Philip IV, king of France
1294–1303	Boniface VIII's pontificate
1300	First papal jubilee
1302	Battle of Courtrai
1305	Papacy transferred to Avignon
1307–1327	Edward II, king of England
1308–1313	Henry VII, emperor of Germany
1314	Battle of Bannockburn
1314–1316	Louis X, king of France
1314–1346	Louis of Bavaria, principal contender for German power and imperial title
1315	Provincial charters of Louis X
1315–1317	Famine throughout Europe
1321	Dante d.
1324	*Defensor pacis* of Marsiglio of Padua
ca. 1327	Meister Eckhart d.
1327–1377	Edward III, king of England
1328–1350	Philip VI, first Valois king of France
1336	Giotto d.
1337	Outbreak of Hundred Years' War
1342	Petrarch, laureate at Rome

1346	Battle of Crécy
1346–1378	Charles IV, emperor of Germany
1347	Cola di Rienzi, tribune at Rome
1348–1349	Black Death
1349	Ockham d.
1350–1364	John II the Good, king of France
1353	*Decameron* of Boccaccio
1353–1363	Restoration of Papal States by Cardinal Albornoz
1354	Rienzi d.
	Ottoman Turks enter Europe
1356	Golden Bull of Charles IV
	Battle of Poitiers
1358	The *Jacquerie*, peasant uprising in France
1360	Peace of Brétigny
ca. 1360	First painted portrait
1364–1380	Charles V the Wise, king of France
1367	Urban V's attempt to return papacy to Rome
1370	Peace of Stralsund
1374	Petrarch d.
1375	Boccaccio d.
1377–1399	Richard II, king of England
1378	Great Schism begun
	Revolt of *Ciompi*, Florence
1378–1400	Wenceslas, emperor of Germany
1380–1422	Charles VI, king of France
1381	Peasants' Revolt in England
1382	Oresme d.
1384	Wyclif d.
1386	Poland and Lithuania united

1396   Turkish defeat of Western crusaders at Nicopolis

1399   Richard II deposed and d.

1400   Wenceslas deposed

1409   Council of Pisa and election of third pope

1410   Battle of Tannenberg

1410–1415   John XXIII, antipope

Suggestions for Further Reading

There is no reliable survey of western Europe in the fourteenth century available in English. Most of the general accounts are of broader scope. Of these, the most recent and the most successful are Denys Hay, *Europe in the Fourteenth and Fifteenth Centuries* (London, 1966), and Wallace K. Ferguson, *Europe in Transition, 1300–1520* (Boston, 1962). Most thorough is Vol. VII of the *Cambridge Medieval History* (Cambridge, 1924–1936). Edward P. Cheney, *The Dawn of a New Era, 1250–1453* (New York, 1936; Torch paperback), makes lively reading and is strong in parts, but has become rapidly outdated, especially in its treatment of economics. A short statement which suggests numerous avenues of investigation is Joseph R. Strayer, "The Promise of the Fourteenth Century," *Proceedings of the American Philosophical Society*, CV (1961), 609–611.

The economic history of the later Middle Ages has recently become an area of heated scholarly debate. The most detailed results of the latest research can be found in the first three volumes of the *Cambridge Economic History of Europe* (Cambridge, 1941–1965), especially in the contributions of Michael M. Postan and Robert S.

Lopez, who emphasize the aspects of depression and decline. An evaluation of the controversy somewhat hostile to the latter two authors is Wallace K. Ferguson, "Recent Trends in the Economic Historiography of the Renaissance," *Studies in the Renaissance*, VII (1960), 7–26. Those who read French should also refer to the recent survey of Jacques Heers, *L'Occident aux xive et xve siècles, aspects économiques et sociaux* (Paris, 1963).

Beyond the last-named work there are not many dependable accounts of the social history of the later Middle Ages. More valuable are special studies of which some of the most interesting in English are David Herlihy, *Pisa in the Early Renaissance* (New Haven, 1958), and Sylvia L. Thrupp, *The Merchant Class of Medieval London* (Chicago, 1948; Ann Arbor paperback). On the pessimistic mood of the later Middle Ages, especially in the North, see Johan Huizinga, *The Waning of the Middle Ages* (London, 1924; Anchor paperback), one of the classics of the literature.

The political history of the Western monarchies is best approached by Alfred Coville and Robert Fawtier, *L'Europe occidentale de 1270 à 1380* (Paris, 1940–1941). For England see the excellent short study of A. R. Myers, *England in the Late Middle Ages* (New York, 1952; Penguin paperback), and the more detailed work of May McKisack, *The Fourteenth Century, 1307–1399* (Oxford, 1959). On France and the Hundred Years' War the best statement is Edouard Perroy, *The Hundred Years' War* (New York, 1965; Capricorn paperback). On Germany the clearest account in English is found in the pertinent chapters of Geoffrey Barraclough, *The Origins of Modern Germany* (Oxford, 1947; Capricorn paperback). The latest study of the fourteenth-century papacy is Guillaume Mollat, *The Popes at Avignon, 1305–1378* (London, 1963; Torch paperback). There is no reliable account of fourteenth-century Italian history in English, but helpful from a more limited point of view is Ferdinand Schevill, *History of Florence* (New York, 1936; Torch paperback, 2 vols., as *Medieval and Renaissance Florence*). Those who wish to extend their view to Spain can still do no better than to read Roger B. Merriman, *The Rise of the Spanish Empire in the Old World and in the New*, Vol. I: *The Middle Ages* (New York, 1918).

On fourteenth-century mysticism see James M. Clark, *The Great German Mystics: Eckhart, Tauler and Suso* (Oxford, 1949); the excellent anthology of Ray C. Petry, *Late Medieval Mysticism* (Philadelphia, 1957); and the fine translation of Raymond B. Blakney, *Meister Eckhart, A Modern Translation* (New York, 1941; Torch paperback).

On radical heresy there is the lively account of Norman Cohn, *The Pursuit of the Millennium* (Fairlawn, 1957; Torch paperback), and on Wyclif, K. B. McFarlane, *John Wycliffe and the Beginnings of English Nonconformity* (London, 1952).

Fine summaries of the work of Ockham and Marsiglio of Padua can be found in Frederick C. Copleston, *Medieval Philosophy* (London, 1952; Torch paperback), and R. L. Poole, *Illustrations of the History of Medieval Thought* (New York, 1920). On Marsiglio see also the recent work of Alan Gewirth, *Marsilius of Padua:*

The Defender of the Peace (2 vols.; New York, 1951–1956), of which the second volume is a translation of Marsiglio's major tract.

Much excellent research has recently been done on the history of mediaeval science. The best summary is A. C. Crombie, *Medieval and Early Modern Science* (2 vols.; New York, 1959; Anchor paperback). A clear account of the fourteenth-century theory of impetus can also be found in the first chapter of Herbert Butterfield, *The Origins of Modern Science* (New York, 1951; Collier paperback). Perhaps the most authoritative survey is provided by Marshall Clagett, *The Science of Mechanics in the Middle Ages* (Madison, 1959).

On technology there is the provocative essay of Lynn T. White, Jr., *Medieval Technology and Social Change* (Oxford, 1962; Oxford paperback), as well as an excellent chapter by A. C. Crombie in the book previously cited. An informative statement about the development of navigation is Frederic C. Lane, "The Economic Meaning of the Invention of the Compass," *American Historical Review*, LXVIII (1963), 605–617.

A brilliant summary of the achievements of the fourteenth-century artists may be found in the early chapters of Erwin Panofsky, *Early Netherlandish Painting, Its Origins and Character* (2 vols.; Cambridge, Mass., 1953). Highly controversial is Frederick Antal, *Florentine Painting and Its Social Background* (London, 1947), which tries to relate stylistic trends to social history. A fascinating study of Italian painting at mid-century is Millard Meiss, *Painting in Florence and Siena after the Black Death* (Princeton, 1951; Torch paperback).

The pathfinding study of Italian vernacular literature is Francesco de Sanctis, *History of Italian Literature* (2 vols.; New York, 1931). Interesting chapters on Dante and Boccaccio which stress the analysis of language and style may be found in Erich Auerbach, *Mimesis* (Princeton, 1953; Anchor paperback). A fascinating account of the development of English is Albert C. Baugh, *A History of the English Language* (New York, 1935).

Two articles describe the new view of history found in Italy. They are Wallace K. Ferguson, "Humanist Views of the Renaissance," *American Historical Review*, XLV (1939), 1–28, and Theodor E. Mommsen, "Petrarch's Conception of the 'Dark Ages,'" *Speculum*, XVII (1942), 226–242.

Index

Agriculture, 17, 18
Albert of Hapsburg, emperor of Germany, 4, 6, 62
Albornoz, cardinal, 74
Anagni, 5
Antwerp, 20
Aquinas, St. Thomas, 82, 84, 92, 110, 111
Aristotle, 98, 99
Avignon, 5, 68, 85

Babylonian Captivity, 74
Bacon, Roger, 98
Ball, John, 27
Bannockburn, battle of, 39
Bardi, 13, 21
Beauvais, cathedral of, 82
Bergen, 22
Black Death, 13-15, 27, 31, 32, 47, 105, 107
Black Prince, 41
Boccaccio, 15, 29, 30, 111, 113, 114, 115
Bohemia, 62, 64, 91
Boniface VIII, pope, 1-6, 36, 37, 67, 108, 120
Bradwardine, Thomas, 98
Bremen, 22
Brétigny, peace of, 56
Bristol, 15
Bruce, Robert, 39, 40, 78
Bruges, 20, 22
Bubonic Plague, see Black Death
Business methods, 23

Calais, 23, 56
Cannon, 102
Capitalism, 23
Catherine of Siena, 86
Charles IV, emperor of Germany, 63, 64
Charles V, king of France, 55-61, 100
Charles VI, king of France, 119, 120
Chaucer, Geoffrey, 30, 115, 116
Chivalry, 29, 30
Ciompi, 24, 25
Clement V, pope, 5
Clement VII, antipope, 74, 75
Clericis laicos, papal bull, 4
Climate, 11
Clocks, 104
Cloth industry, 19, 20
Constance, Council of, 120
Courtrai, battle of, 24
Crécy, battle of, 40, 55, 57, 102
Curia regis, 42, 43

Dancers, 32, 33
Dante, 3, 30, 63, 110-113, 117
Dawson, Christopher, 28
Devotia moderna, 87
Dolcino, 26

Eckhart, 84-86
Economic alliances, 21-23
Economic crisis, 7-23

Edward I, king of England, 4, 6, 36, 37, 39, 45, 49, 54, 96
Edward II, king of England, 37-39, 41, 42, 46
Edward III, king of England, 37, 39-41, 45, 52-56, 60
England, 37-48, 78, 89-91
Estates-General, 57-60
Eyeglasses, 105

Famine of 1315, 10, 11
Fine arts, 105-109
Firearms, 102
Flagellants, 31, 32
Flanders, 20, 24, 26, 54
Floods, 11
Florence, 3, 11, 14, 24, 25, 72, 78, 107, 110
France, 24, 26, 27, 40-42, 48-61, 68, 77, 78, 114
Free Spirit, heresy of, 32, 33, 88, 89
Froissart, Jean, 114, 116

Garter, order of, 30
Gascony, 53, 54, 56
Gaveston, Piers, 38, 39
Germany, 21, 48, 61-67, 86, 87
Giotto, 1, 3, 106, 107, 110, 111, 117
Golden Bull, 64
Great Ordinance, 58
Great Schism, 74-76
Gregory XI, pope, 74
Grosseteste, Robert, 98
Guesclin, Bertrand du, 56, 57
Gunpowder, 102

Halidon Hill, battle of, 40
Hamburg, 22
Hanse, 21, 22
Hapsburgs, 65, 66
Henry VII, emperor of Germany, 62, 63, 70
Henry of Lancaster, 43
Heraldry, 29, 30
Hohenzollerns, 65, 66
Hospitalers, 50
House of Commons, 45, 46, 59

House of Lords, 46
Hundred Years' War, 26, 30, 40-42, 53-57, 77, 78, 114
Hus, John, 91

Impetus, theory of, 99, 100
International Style, 108
Ireland, 42
Isabella, queen of England, 39, 40
Italy, 20, 24, 25, 26, 62, 63, 67-73

Jacquerie, 26, 27, 58
John XXIII, antipope, 76
John of Jandun, 94
John the Good, king of France, 55, 56, 58, 109
Jubilee, papal, 1-4
Justice of the peace, 47, 48

Lithuania, 65
Lollards, 91
London, 22, 27, 28
Longbow, 54, 55
Louis IX, king of France, 48
Louis X, king of France, 51
Louis of Bavaria, emperor of Germany, 63, 69, 94
Lübeck, 22
Luxembourgers, 65, 66

Map-making, 103
Marcel, Etienne, 58, 59
Mariner's compass, 103
Marsiglio of Padua, 94-96
Matins of Bruges, 24
Medici, 72
Medicine, 105
Merton College, 98
Milan, 71
Mining industry, 18
Mongols, 11, 12
Morgarten, battle of, 65
Mysticism, 84-87

Naples, 70
Nationalism, 77
Natural science, 96-101
Neoplatonism, 85

Nicopolis, battle of, 12
Nogaret, Guillaume de, 5
Nominalism, 91-101, 107
Novgorod, 22

Ockham, William of, 92-94, 98
Oresme, Nicolas of, 100, 101
Ottoman Turks, 12
Oxford, 97, 98

Paris, 98-101, 107
Parliament, 44-47
Pastoureaux, 11, 26
Peasants' Revolt of 1381, 27, 28
Perspective, 105, 106
Peruzzi, 13, 21
Petrarch, 73, 111-113, 115-117
Philip IV, the Fair, king of
   France, 4-6, 36, 37, 48-51, 54,
   57, 60, 96
Philip VI, king of France, 52-55
Pisa, Council of, 75-76
Poitiers, battle of, 40, 55, 58
Political theory, 94-96
Portrait, 108, 109
Prussia, 65
Pucelle, Jean, 107, 108

Quarter Sessions, 48

Reims, 60
Richard II, king of England, 28,
   37, 41-43
Rienzi, 73
Robin Hood, 26, 47
Rome, 72-74, 113
Rostock, 22
Ruysbroeck, Jan, 86, 87

Salic Law, 52
Scotland, 38-40

Shipbuilding, 102, 103
Siena, 14, 107
Social status, 29-31
Social upheaval, 23-31
Spiritual Franciscans, 70
Staple, 22, 23
Stralsund, peace of, 22
Sumptuary laws, 29
Suso, Heinrich, 85-87
Switzerland, 64, 65

Tamerlaine, 12
Tannenberg, battle of, 65
Tauler, Johann, 85-87
Technology, 101-105
Tell, William, 65, 78
Templars, 49, 50
Teutonic Knights, 65
Thessalonica, 25
Trade routes, contraction of, 11,
   12
Tyler, Wat, 28

Unam sanctam, papal bull, 4, 5
Urban V, pope, 74
Urban VI, pope, 74

Valois dynasty, 52
Venice, 71
Vernacular literature, 86, 91, 109-
   116
Villani, Giovanni, 3, 116
Visconti family, 71

Wenceslas, emperor of Germany,
   64, 119, 120
Wismar, 22
Woolen industry, 19
Wyclif, John, 89-91, 96

Ypres, 20